Shattered Glass

From Victim to Survivor

VICTORIA COURT

Published by

MELROSE
BOOKS

An Imprint of Melrose Press Limited
St Thomas Place, Ely
Cambridgeshire
CB7 4GG, UK
www.melrosebooks.com

FIRST EDITION

Cover designed by Nikki Bovis-Coulter

ISBN 1 905226 70 5

Printed and bound in Great Britain by:
CPI Antony Rowe, Bumpers Farm,
Chippenham, Wiltshire, SN14 6LH, UK

All names, locations and dates have been changed to protect identity.

Where the word 'friends' is used in the generic sense, no individuals are pinpointed.

Foreword – From Victim to Survivor

This is a story with no completion to date, with questions left unanswered and decisions left unmade. This is my true account, written initially for my therapy only, but which I believe God wants me to share with others who may be on the same road. I want you to know you are not alone in this roller-coaster ride that is the journey from victim to survivor of domestic violence. And yes, I am a survivor, in that I have escaped, alive, from a marriage that could have left me as a murder statistic.

Some people think you shouldn't use the word 'victim' in relation to domestic violence since it indicates a lack of hope and despair, something already being instilled into a women by her abuser. 'Survivor', in the context in which I am able to use it right now, refers simply to someone who has left the abusive relationship and is starting the frightening journey to rebuild her life. If you are still a victim, this doesn't mean you can't have a capacity for survival within it, in the same way as a survivor may be suffering from all types of trauma. For some of us, survival has previously meant just staying alive in the face of violence.

I do not pretend to be one hundred per cent recovered, and, as I write, I am still left with chronic symptoms of post-traumatic stress. Some would tell me to recover and become a 'real' survivor (however you may interpret that) before I share my story with you, but I want you to know it as it is, and learn whatever it is that God wants you to learn from what I am writing. At the moment there is no '... And she lived happily ever after ...' but there is "... For I know the plans I have for you, says the Lord, plans to prosper you and not to harm you, plans to give you a hope and a future …" (Jeremiah 29 v 11)

So come with me on my journey, a journey from danger to the promises of hope I could not be making without God as my constant companion and guardian, in a situation where many, myself included at times, would question, 'Lord, if you're there … why?'

The Bible is full of journeys - imagine Abraham, called by God to leave his country and travel to an unknown place that God would show him. Think of his fears - where was he going? Why? Would he meet enemies? Would there be battles on the way? Would the land God was promising be better than where he was living now, settled and secure?

I do not claim to know all the answers but I know who holds the future, and I know that He has a plan for every experience, however pointless it may seem at the time; so come with me on the beginning of my journey - the journey from victim to survivor.

I grew up in a Christian family that was poor materially but rich in every other way. I understood about my parents' beliefs from as far back as I remember but found my own faith and relationship with God when I was only seven, and realised when I was a few years older that I needed Him as my saviour, and my faith and church took on a new meaning: one that included a deep love and forgiveness, and became of central importance.

In my situation today, these principles, whilst remaining absolutely true, can cause confusion in the best of churches, as a woman who has, for nearly five years, lived my secret and shameful life: that of a victim of domestic violence. Whilst every human being is unique in God's eyes, we still live in a physical world with physical rules where there is a necessary difference between being caught up in a sinful world and making an active choice to commit a criminal offence. This can cause much heartache and confusion within the Church, whose work centres around the message of forgiveness, especially when the situation is new to them and they initially may desperately want to support both victim and perpetrator.

I grew up (not because this is how I was told to think, but because this is just the person I am) wanting a career, but also top of my list was a little girl's dream of a handsome prince, loving and protecting me, and of having children – an 'and they lived happily ever after' story.

As I write today, I'm only thirty-four, have a deteriorating disability, and my dream lies in tatters. If I had to represent my life, right now, in one photograph, it would be of a beautiful picture, which you cannot see through shattered glass. The glass is me, and the picture is my dream, which was once a dream, and now is a dream again, but this time, right now, an unattainable one. In fact, in my marriage it was never anything but a dream, but like many women, once an attack was over, I knew it would 'just' be the psychological and emotional abuse for the next few days or weeks until the next assault. I tried to 'behave better', I blamed myself, I thought I should try harder, I was told I was mad and it was all my fault, and I trusted him, so he must be right. In the in-between times you can pretend life is always this 'good', although for me eventually, the 'good' was the lack of abuse, so low had my expectations sunk. I had made my vows, and as a Christian had said publicly 'for better or worse'.

What about the church?

Well, I am thrilled to say that the first thing my minister said to me, when the situation was disclosed to him via a counsellor who had to break my confidence, was that I had not broken my wedding vows, that my husband had broken them in the world's eyes and in God's the first time he ever abused me. That was such a relief. The main minister and his wife, along with countless members of my loving church family have been nothing but supportive and loving of me, and have said that when I hear it preached that people should try to keep their marriages together under any circumstances, they are not referring to me or anyone in an abusive situation. I've been so thankful for that.

However, this makes me ask: how many churchgoers out there have ever heard the words 'domestic violence' mentioned publically? Statistically in my church there will be at least another ten women suffering in silence, and possibly thinking they have to endure it simply because it just isn't mentioned, and things that aren't mentioned are usually condoned!

How thankful I was that my minister said he was more concerned about my emotional wellbeing than where my husband would have to worship if and when I could take no more. He gave me the family's home phone number and said that he or his wife or son would pick me up any time of day or night in an emergency.

I have recently had the courage to take out an injunction against my husband. I had really thought that God might use this to help him see the error of his ways, but, like the vast majority of abusers, he is in denial. Some Christians have even said that I should press charges if I love him, as time in prison or better still, on a perpetrator course, might force him into thinking. Maybe I love him too much – maybe I don't love him enough – right now I'm too mixed up to know, but when I envisage him in a courtroom, I see those gentle eyes, the 'made up' ones in my imagination, the 'public eyes' which changed the second we were private and committed, then I can't bear to hurt him, even though I know that he has tried to ruin my life and someone else's before me.

The church still loves and supports me, and were it not for many friends of different ages who witnessed what I call very minor things, I would probably still be living in danger as a victim, since it was only when other people asked me whether I was okay that I started to ask those questions myself. Some people were shocked, but most could see it in retrospect. Several friends had advised me to keep a record of incidents (which I was already doing) and have a bag packed and in the car. My minister also advised me this. Only I could ultimately make the decisions I have made and will make in the future, in the same way that only Robert could choose to behave how he did towards me, but many people have helped me to have some insight into my relationship, which I appreciated in different ways at different times.

So many friends have supported me; in fact, one church worker said that 'hearts were breaking' over me and the whole situation, which made me feel valued in a situation where the emotional abuse has robbed me of all self-worth and esteem, to the point where, despite the love I feel, I have also felt like an appendix even in the body of the church!

People do feel out of their depth – it is obvious, with respect, that some will acknowledge this and some will not. Although I have no doubts of sincere love, care and support, I need people to be understanding and to be willingly educated. I feel that I have a dirty secret which I'm not allowed to share, and, completely unintentionally, the things I suffered at the hands of my abuser – shame, filth, blame, guilt, self-hatred, the list is endless – are, at times, reinforced by this feeling that I am alone in my secret club which is too unsavoury to be discussed in church or elsewhere.

It is fair to say that I am suffering, as I believe all women who escape do, to some extent, from post-traumatic stress and depression, and I know that I am not always behaving as the real me. In fact, the real me was nearly destroyed in my marriage so I am waiting to rediscover myself! However, I do know when God has blessed me through things I see or hear in church.

After one service very recently, I really felt that God wanted me to share what He had done for me by ultimately keeping me safe. I had no plans, let alone the courage, to go into gruesome details, only to tell how I had been moved by the service, realising once again, as I already know deep down all the time, that I am special to God. I spoke to a couple of people who were in charge that day (the senior minister wasn't there at the time), who told me I 'wasn't ready'. In fact, when I said I was so thankful that I was still alive I was told 'not to exaggerate' by someone I'd never spoken to before! (I am glad to say he represents a very small minority, and has since understood.) I knew then for certain that it wasn't me who wasn't ready – it was the church. Was Paul's jailor in the Bible ready to be baptised the second he heard the good news? Or was he told he wasn't ready? Did Jesus tell the 'unsavoury, mad' men to go and tell everybody what he had done for them, or did he tell them they weren't ready?

A very small minority of the leadership team who, of course, do not necessarily always reflect 'the Church', let alone God, have just confirmed (albeit non-verbally) that yes, I do have a dirty secret that mustn't be let out. But I need to be patient too, because I have been on this road much longer than they have, and they are still in a state of shock.

This is why this opportunity is such a blessing – when God speaks to us, and we feel we want to share, then we *are* ready, whether or not people want to hear.

I have struggled with what appears to be today's views in many churches similar to mine, that church discipline is no longer within their remit, unlike most secular places who would immediately take action. This has caused me great fear about attending church and public places in general, and also distress and spiritual confusion which is an added challenge that caused, for a time, more depression than the abuse itself, that now I must work through. A lovely lady at church, who is very wise and whose husband had been in a pastoral position for many years, slipped a piece of paper into my hands just after I had seen them once about my situation. I still carry it in my purse with me today – it simply says, "What we permit, we promote." I can't help feeling this applies to the church too, and my ongoing prayer is that Christian churches will become places of refuge and safe havens for women living with, fleeing from, and living with the after-effects of domestic violence.

There are many myths about domestic violence and a

particularly 'comfortable' one is that men are mentally ill, and this is an argument I have been faced with within the church and elsewhere. I suppose it sanitises it. In reality, it is too widespread to be explained away by this. Most men confine violence to their own homes and are not a danger to anyone else. Abuse is often aimed at parts of the body that are covered or will not visibly mark. I have been in the middle of an assault, my husband has picked up the phone and had a normal conversation, put the phone down and carried on where he left off. That is called a choice. Yes, he is ill in the way that as a Christian, I believe we all are – it's the unpopular word sin! Apart from that, he has no excuse.

Obviously, I have been in my secret club, alone, for years, so I have moved comparatively quickly through this 'shock stage', having known about it all along, but maybe others are still numb. Rob was thankfully dissuaded from attending the church and withdrew his membership when the time came for it to be taken from him. Many people are in a state of shock from realising what further implications this whole situation may have. I had never really accounted for the ripple effects for other people. I just knew how fantastic life was, and how I returned to the real, bubbly me whenever he was away for weekends – and I think it is challenging but important for women to know that it is not just safety issues that change on separation. I know I am currently over-sensitive and may (and do repeatedly) easily misinterpret things. I know I have over-burdened people; I know I have gone into what has, to me, been minor, but others have considered excessive detail that has unnecessarily upset and shocked people – something else which I can add to my 'guilt list'. I think people find it confusing that I look so much better, and at times I am the happy, bubbly person they used to know. But at other times I suddenly 'slip away' back into my horror world where only I can ever be and where no one can come with me, except God. And I have to remember that He was there, in every situation, at every attack, in all the pain, in all the hurt. He could have stopped it, but chose not too, but I know this is because there is a reason that I may not yet know. I want to be able to help educate Christians in the future, so that people can come forward and we can start to live in a world free from violence against women. It wasn't many years ago that I belonged to the 'I'd never let a man hurt me, and if he did, I'd only allow him to get away with it once' brigade. If you've not been there you can never understand fully. That's why I believe as a Christian that once I've recovered I cannot leave behind the lessons I have learned through this – I must use them to help transform the lives of other women.

On that Sunday when I was stopped from sharing what God has done for me, I read these words, and it is as though they are written especially for me, whose self-esteem has probably been affected more than anything else:

> "Faith is: Remembering I am indispensable to God when I feel I only clutter up the landscape!
> Remembering I am God's priceless treasure when I feel utterly worthless
> Confidence in God's faithfulness to me in an uncertain world, on an uncharted course, through an unknown future."
>
> ('Faith is', Pamela Reeve)

I believe that, despite initial ups and downs, I have been blessed by having a church that has coped as well as it has, and remembering that the church is made up of fallible humans; but we are only at the very beginning of a very long road that I hope they will want to follow, not just for me, but for others both now and in the future. We follow so carefully, and to the letter, our policy on working with children and young people, and my prayer is that we will be prepared to protect all vulnerable people, whether we find it savoury or not. I also have to keep reminding myself that I follow God, not the church, and God's ways are always right and always perfect.

Throughout my journey, as I have only discovered many months on, the church has also been learning, studying and recognising domestic violence more and more. They have been on their own journey too, and I pray that one day we will become a 'role model' church, ready to accept and manage many challenging situations. Many have moved miles since I started writing, and I thank God for the leaders and members who have become survivors of 'unsavoury' topics with me! It is now mentioned in talks and prayers, and secret meetings take place in the ladies' toilets at times!! There is even a domestic violence policy that has appeared on the notice board. It is easy to forget that we only learn about things we come into contact with, and if my experiences have helped, and will help others, then I believe they can be used to glorify God who has a reason for everything, however difficult it may be to see it at the time.

Throughout my journey, I have been helped enormously by specialist domestic outreach services; I often think that I would never have started the journey to freedom, nor be here today without them, and I am so very thankful that such services exist.

My sincere and unending thanks goes to them and also to the Baptist Union of Great Britain for their help both to me personally and in helping to educate the church, and for their permission to reproduce some of their materials.

If any of this strikes a chord with you, or you want to learn more, then there are several addresses and telephone numbers at the back of this book, the top two being the main and largest providers of outreach support and refuge accommodation in the UK.

Acknowledgements

The author and publisher would like to acknowledge the following copyrights:

For all excerpts from *Praying Our Goodbyes* –

Praying Our Goodbyes by Joyce Rupp, OSM. Copyright ©1992 by Ave Maria Press, P.O. Box 428, Notre Dame, Indiana, 46556, www.avemariapress.com. Used with permission of the publisher.

For the extract taken from the song *In Christ Alone* by Keith Getty and Stuart Townend –

*Adm. by worshiptogether.com songs excl. UK & Europe, adm. by kingswaysongs.com tym@kingsway.co.uk Used by permission.

Contents

Introduction
February 2002 – Me

This book is dedicated to my first counsellor, Gill, who first made me realise that I could be a survivor, and to Ali, the first and main person from the specialist women's outreach service who helped me put it into practice, by carrying, then empowering me, and then by 'pushing me out of the nest' with wings which will always be there in some form until I no longer need them.

I have lived with domestic violence, domestic abuse, woman abuse, wife abuse, whatever you want to call it, for four and a half years to date. Most people will call it whatever they think sanitises it the most.

As I secretly begin to write the initial draft I am still living as a victim. I have subtitled this book 'from victim to survivor' because although I am still allowing myself to be a victim I have a pact with myself and with God, who made me in His image, (one that He doesn't want deliberately and constantly destroyed), that one day soon I shall become a survivor.

The Christian message is one of healing and hope for the hurting. Throughout the Bible the message is that situations can be turned around and good made out of bad.

I know that becoming a survivor will not happen at the moment of separation, and I still cling to the hope that I may become a survivor and remain in my marriage, but, even as a Christian who believes in miracles, I recognise the naivety of that hope. Maybe it is that which is helping me take that first stumbling, childlike step from victim to survivor by writing this account.

I was born in 1971 into a family who loved, cherished and valued me, and, thirty-four years on, the days on which I don't communicate somehow with them that I love them are few and far between.

We grew up on the breadline, but a very happy breadline, had hours and hours of quality time, pursued many hobbies, such as arts and crafts with my mum, and growing vegetables and helping on the allotment with my dad, and reading and, above all, loads of imaginative play with the many friends in our neighbourhood. As a teacher now, I can see that our upbringing was a teacher's dream – ironically the lack of money caused the prerequisites for acquiring not only academic but play skills involving negotiation, compromise, empathy and such like.

I grew up in a Baptist church, one of the stricter types to which I would never return but which gave me a good solid grounding in so many aspects of life that I would never regret it. They were invariably happy times with many people who cared about me and provided a large peer group around me.

I understood the real meaning of faith at just seven years old and at the age of nine I made a commitment to follow God and serve Him for the rest of my life on the basis of understanding my own need for a saviour as a sinner caught up in a world full of people choosing to go their own way without Him. I experienced in both heart and mind the reality of the love of God and the lengths He had gone to for me on the cross, and that is what makes me an eternal survivor whatever I may face in this world.

At the age of seven I remember a verse that meant a great deal to me. I was going to the dentist to have some teeth out, but at the time this was a very frightening ordeal for me. On our kitchen calendar that day it read: "My heart trusted in Him and I am helped." Psalm 28:7. All I wanted and needed to know at that time was that God would help me open my mouth at the dentist!

I can understand now why God wants us, wants me, to

have a childlike faith.

The big lesson I am constantly struggling to learn right now, is that when we step out in faith we may only see step one.

I still want to see steps two, three, four, five and so on; I want to know:

- If I leave, will I marry again or will I be alone forever?
- Do I want to marry again? Supposing it happens again? Do I attract abusive men?
- Will I have to move? (The house is about to be adapted for me as I'm disabled and my energy levels are frightening low and my pain levels intolerably high at times.)
- What about children?
- Why aren't I a mum already – God knows it's all I've ever really wanted. I feel I'm destined for 'the shelf', and even if not, then time is getting shorter.
- Will I be able to adopt?
- Will they consider me 'appropriate' as a disabled single parent?
- Will people believe me?
- Will my friends stand by me as promised?
- Am I really mad? Is everything he says about me true?

I remember the quite old fashioned but meaningful words I learned in Sunday school:

"God holds the key of all unknown and I am glad,
If other hands should hold the key, or if He trusted it to me,
I might be sad, I might be sad.

I cannot read His future plans, but this I know,
I have the smiling of His face, and all the refuge of His grace,
While here below, while here below.

What if tomorrow's cares were here, without its rest?

I'd rather He unlocked the day, and as the hours swing open say,
'My will is best, my will is best'.

And so, this covers all my wants, and so I rest!
For what I cannot, He can see, and in his care I safe shall be,
Forever blessed, Forever blessed."

(Joseph Parker 1830–1902)

My sister, who is two years younger than me, married in 1995. In many ways we are chalk and cheese but are really best friends.

The year my sister was married, the strange and undiagnosed problems that concerned my parents increasingly throughout my life were finally diagnosed as neurological after a more obvious decline in my ability to walk, write, balance and coordinate. I had always had problems that had been a nuisance and I had had difficulties with back and joint pain since adolescence. I'd also been born with a club foot which it had not been possible to correct. I had a diagnosis from a local neurologist who confirmed this in early 1996 as (then) very mild generalised dystonia. This is a condition in which people get sustained and twisted muscle contractions and spasms causing abnormal movements and bizarre postures. In some cases, mine included, the pain can be excruciating. It is progressive but not degenerative.

Six years on it is considered severe and affects my entire skeleton, and also the muscles around other internal organs. I have tried numerous medicines – many with awful side effects, but I did get relief from one powerful muscle relaxant, alongside other muscle relaxants, plus an increasingly powerful cocktail of opiates. After we got engaged I very slowly stopped the main drug as we were united, I thought, in our desire to have children. We had been to one of the national neurological hospitals and had listened as the consultant had explained the probable effects of stopping this drug – maybe I would be unable to work, probably unable to walk.

More recently, my pain levels have increased terribly and I have become less stable on my feet. Even major pioneering brain surgery has been suggested. Like any condition, especially neurological, stress is an exacerbating feature. I have started tripping regularly, necessitating further hospital appointments and numerous consultants. As I write I am awaiting an assessment from the community rehabilitation team for the house, as the stairs are becoming dangerous for me on grounds of disability alone, let alone the odd 'helping hand' in the form of a shove or 'accidental' push. I have never been 'allowed' adaptations or even to use my wheelchair, which has caused me to be a prisoner in my own home as time has gone on.

However, in some ways I am already a survivor of my disability and it forms a large part of my story as I encroach upon my tale of trying to escape from being a victim of domestic abuse.

My lifelong calling, since the age of six, has been to teach children with special needs. Every medical I have had since my own schooldays has threatened to 'blow' my career out of the water before it even started, yet I knew that God had this special calling for my life and for nearly thirteen years I have been teaching children with severe learning difficulties, even working with some of the most challenging pupils. Even the fact that the school have employed a full-time support worker to help me do the hands-on stuff in school is proof of God and His goodness shown through the fantastic friends and colleagues I work with – when this seems so unlikely on human terms. I am still doing what many people would shy away from. So, maybe I do have the potential to be a survivor after all!

I would like, right at the beginning, to thank the people who have helped and are helping me to move from victim to survivor. I couldn't do it without them and 'thanks' seems so insufficient. Above all I acknowledge the undeserved and always patient, unending love of God, who is the saviour in the lives of many of these people:

For my mum, who I tried to keep in the dark but who knew anyway because she knows and loves me so well. However, she didn't know the complete truth until six weeks before it all ended; Rob thought I told her everything - but then he had no idea of the protectiveness of love. I always swore that once she knew it would be the end - she couldn't cope with wondering constantly what was happening to me. I had seen the effects on my friends, some of whom appear to this day to have 'secondary' post-traumatic stress, so how could I do this to my own mum, who'd do anything for me?

For my sister who first saw me flinch and cared enough to challenge me and contact my friends, and for her wisdom and practical help throughout, even though she's my 'baby sister'.

For many good Christian friends, some of my age, some older and even wiser, some who spoke to my sister and have been a constant support and refuge in times of trouble and calmer times, and whom, without, I couldn't have gone on. Several even cared enough to set up a system of 'safe words' for my protection and as part of my safety plan.

For our minister who married us and who met with Gill and I, and who showed an understanding and concern that was a great encouragement to me. Special and ongoing thanks to him and his wife, who have put up with my endless distressed e-mails, letters and phone calls and who have been prepared to help (despite being untrained specifically in this area); and for their love even when I feel that my problems have selfishly put them out of their depth, and I've given them a hard time (and I certainly have!) and must have seemed ungrateful! This must be so difficult when domestic violence is 'new' to you. (I should add in here, in my final draft, that I am now a proud member of a church that is more understanding, completely intolerant of, and prepared to stand up and speak out against domestic violence publicly, and that most people who initially found the situation so challenging are being restored and rebuilt, along with me, both close friends, new friends, fellow members and acquaintances.)

For my fantastic friends and ex-pastors, who just knew from several hundred miles away that something was amiss, and who have since supported, loved, prayed and advised me most wisely from afar as both best friends and pastors. And for their co-workers here in Devon; my pastor and his wife who never saw anything, myself included, as a 'job', but as a ministry.

For the concern and time of the medical profession and the little and unbeknown ways in which they have helped me; especially my physio, who has done so much out of the call of duty and has been patient enough to listen to my 'stuck record', whenever I've needed someone 'professional', yet friendly to be there for me. She, like so many other people who are not mentioned here, probably has no idea as to the important significance of her role in my 'disclosure' and healing processes. I am so fortunate to have a strong network, and realise with gratitude that whatever I have been through, I have not been completely alone, even though no human can travel with me to the darkest places I have been.

For my very best colleague and teaching assistant of eleven years, who went as my envoy to explain my apparent 'personality change' to my boss, and to him for his extreme understanding, patience and offer of a baseball bat (though I declined, thanks all the same!) He has been a constant support since, along with some good male medics, police officers and friends – I feel that this should not go unrecognised in my world, where I don't want to 'tar all men with the same brush'.

And especially for my two specialist outreach workers, whom I wish I'd met years ago, for listening to me going on like a stuck record, for being patient when all I wanted to do was to run myself down and couldn't look at goals for my future. Neither share my faith as far as I know, but the first seemed at the time like an angel sent to rescue me, the second helped me put into practice the things in this book I knew to be true in my mind a long time before I could really feel them in my heart; they would tell me I have helped myself – but it will always be true that they empowered me, and I couldn't have done it without them. They have been totally indispensable in this journey. Never assume God can only use those who share your beliefs – whatever they may be! I have to be honest and say, however much they refuse to take the credit; that I'm not certain I would be here today if it weren't for them.

It has come to my attention in all too hard a way that the Church in general, with the best will in the world, doesn't 'do' domestic violence. I am fortunate to have a church that will not take the stance that I must stay and be abused – my marriage vows have already been broken by the violence and desertion and God's image in me is being slowly destroyed. As I write I feel like a hollow shell, all scooped out, with the real me dead somewhere, but this doesn't mean that they know how to handle it. In fact, right from the moment of disclosure, they encouraged me to leave, at least temporarily, to see what happened – but this brief parting met initially with charm and then the cycle continued as it always had.

Churches 'do' marriage problems, they 'do' affairs, they 'do' bereavement, they 'do' crises of conscience or faith, they 'do' meetings on what colour the toilets should be painted, but they don't 'do' domestic violence. It's just not sanitary for a church, and this isn't an issue of blame – it's more to do with not recognising that there are those of us who suffer and keep quiet when we know we shouldn't.

It is taking me a while to learn that what God says counts, and where this doesn't fit in with the Church, which is overseen by human beings, then it is God who we must listen to and obey.

I dedicate this book to the many Christians and other friends without whose love and concern I would probably not be here to tell the tale, but I also feel that as well as being autobiographical, they need to be educated in the most basic facts. On average, one in four women experiences domestic violence at some point in their lives. That doesn't necessarily mean severe, ongoing and almost 'ritualistic' as it was for me, but it's still a frightening figure.

Many people call Christians hypocrites, but hypocrites are those who claim to have it right, and I know few, if any, people who would claim this. Whilst these statistics are likely to be lower in an evangelical church (apparently, statistically still one in seven), in a church of five hundred people like mine, I am highly unlikely to be the only Christian woman being 'beaten into submission'. It may be that you're not being hurt physically, and can hide it really well - even from yourself - it's not just the abusers who are into denial.

This book is also for all of you too: for victim number three who is still in the dark, for friends who think abuse is okay unless you are in actual physical danger; friends who think it's okay if there are long times in between which are loving and enjoyable; people who are still living as victims, or survivors, or, whether you're like me, praying that by God's grace, you are on the way to survival.

And, in that strange, twisted way that you will only understand if you've been in my 'secret club', I dedicate this book to the two men who were my husband: my precious husband and my terrifying abuser, who is still as yet the only person for whom I would give my life ... and nearly did.

Chapter One
From Victim to Survivor

11th June 1999

'Will you keep your b***** head on your side of the bed! You're a selfish cow and you never think of things from my point of view.'

SHOVE.

My neck involuntarily moved back – my spine is not a straight line – not a new concept – it had been like that since we first met. I suffer from generalised dystonia, a rare neurological movement disorder causing involuntary movements, bizarre postures and extreme pain.

SHOVE (a bit harder this time, warranted by the fact that I was being 'awkward').

'I can't help it.'

SHOVE.

'You're just being awkward – you always have to have the last word.' Back went my neck and spine, crossing that midline marked so neatly (and ironically with a heart on the headboard) on the bed, lest I forget and accidentally cross it at any point during the night.

SHOVE.

'You're hurting me.'

SHOVE.

'You're an awkward, selfish b**** and you just can't be told. You're an absolute nightmare – you're worse than your predecessor.'

SHOVE.

I tried to get up and move so I could go to the other bed – it was uncomfortable but maybe I could creep back when he was asleep; he's such a sound sleeper. I tried to get up. I was fearful as usual, which made my movements more uncoordinated and awkward. I got myself semi-upright – not quick enough –

SHOVE.

'I'm going.' I sat up on the edge of the bed, got myself upright and managed to walk shakily to the end of his side of the bed where I slumped on the corner. I was coming off my drugs so that we could start a family and was suffering from frequent 'whole body' spasms as a reaction.

SHOVE.

This time it was from behind. I was exhausted.

SHOVE and maybe a kick – no, not 'officially' a kick, just a hard push with the legs, hard enough to throw me off the mattress to the floor at the end of the bed.

'Don't try and frighten me. You only do it for effect.'

I lay there and shook from head to toe. I didn't have my 'old lady's' lifeline pendant on me (I feel wary of cords around my neck), so I was quite helpless. I could feel a dystonic 'storm' coming on and was trembling violently. It was so cold.

'If you won't help me up, please cover me with a dressing gown,' I called as I lay stuck backwards in a spasm on the floor at the end of the bed.

NO ANSWER.

I pleaded several times and noticed from the clock that over an hour had elapsed and I decided not to humiliate myself with further begging, no matter how much I hurt from the cold. (Shivering, as well he knew, caused some of the worst pains.)

I decided to try and move; my pulse had been racing with fear and I was desperate for the loo. I pulled myself along the floor slowly and surely, desperately trying not to fuss and make things worse, but vainly letting out the odd moan, cajoling myself that I could make it past his side of the bed, where I thought he was asleep, and to the en suite. Eventually I got there and rested my sore spasming neck against the cold edge of the sink.

'I've had enough of this.' He tried to pick me up off the loo, but the spasms were so strong they were even defeating an angry fifteen stoner. On the second attempt he made it, picked me up and threw me onto the bed. Now my neck was stuck backwards and my eyes clamped shut - not the most enviable state when faced with a man acting like a psychopath.

'I want to discuss it.' (Discuss what? I thought.)

'You're just pretending, stop trying to scare me, you're so awkward.' No response. My jaw had clamped shut as well as my eyes (fairly unusual for me back then, as anyone who knows me will vouch!).

The next thing I knew was a pint cold glass of water straight in my face, wetting my pillow and bedding. Then the smash of glass very near me. My eyes were still shut and I couldn't see.

He got me a towel to lie on where the bed was soaked and then proceeded to hoover the bedroom.

'Honestly, woman, you're not in your right mind - you are a mess.'

Ten minutes later, and he was snoring like a baby.

This was just a variation on my normal weekend routine.

16th June 1999

At last! The long awaited text message - 'Ouch! It's really happening - going in soon!'

The next day I met my precious niece for the very first time, so perfect and so loved after the initial shock and fear of motherhood. I expected to feel jealousy as well as love, but when I saw the bond of love that had so instantly formed, apparently out of nowhere, I felt nothing but pride (although I still hoped it would be me very soon!). It was ironic - my sister had never before that moment really wanted much to do with children - (she's changed now!) and I've always dreamed of nothing else.

Sunday 25th June 1999

I stood there singing along with the rest of them. I have always enjoyed singing and this new song was turning out to be a favourite.

"In Christ alone, my hope is found, He is my light, my strength, my song
This solid ground, this cornerstone, firm through the fiercest drought and storm,
What heights of love, what depths of peace, when fears are stilled, when strivings cease,

My comforter, my all in all, here in the love of Christ I stand.

In Christ alone, who took on flesh, fullness of God in helpless babe,
This gift of love and righteousness, scorned by the ones He came to save,
Til on that cross, as Jesus died, the wrath of God was satisfied,
When every sin on Him was laid, here in the death of Christ I live.

There in the ground His body lay, light of the world by darkness slain,
Then bursting forth to glorious day, up from the grave He rose again,
And as He stands in victory, sin's curse has lost its grip on me,

For I am His, and He is mine, bought with the precious blood of Christ.

No guilt in life, no fear in death, this is the power of Christ in me,
From lifes first cry to final breath, Jesus commands my destiny …
No power of hell, No scheme of man, can ever pluck me from His hands,
Til He returns or calls me home, Here in the love of Christ I stand."

Extract taken from the song
"In Christ Alone" by Keith Getty and Stuart Townsend.

The tears streamed down my face – the words 'hit home' as they could never have done before. The words are enough to move anyone but that week I had faced both life's first cry and what in my fear may have been my final breath.

But I know who's in control, I know who commands my destiny and that terror can never come between me and the Lord even when I felt that my actual breath could be strangled out of me.

I think this was the exact moment I realised that I could no longer live in denial – I was still madly in love, but also a victim of domestic violence and maybe I could still hide it, but I was too tired and too frightened to run anymore.

That same week I heard an advert on the radio as I was driving home from work. I'd never heard it before, but as soon as it started I somehow knew what the ending would be, and it helped to set me on my journey to get help … help that was to change my whole life. The advert went something like this: "For thousands of women in Britain today, this is the most frightening sound they will hear." I immediately knew that that sound would be the sound of keys turning in the lock – and I swerved over into a lay-by, shaking and faint, just before the advert finished … and there was the sound of those keys turning in the lock … followed by that phone number that was to start my journey.

Chapter Two

10th April 2001

Tonight I really, really want to text Rob to tell him how much I love him and miss him and to check that he's okay. I feel as though I've never loved him as much. But however much I want, I need, to text him, I won't, because I have taken a big step towards freedom, and am rediscovering that I can be in control.

Exactly two weeks and five days ago I got an ex parte injunction with power of arrest against Robert.

We'd been together five years and twenty-one days.

We'd been married three years, one month and seventeen days (although I am still married and he is still my husband, the only man for me).

Sorry if domestic violence is a 'new' thing to you and this makes you feel confused or uncomfortable, but that's how it is – for all of us, for a long time – that is just one of the many 'unsavoury' challenges of living with a violent partner. Even a publisher told me that it was 'too difficult' to read, because it was uncomfortable how I still had feelings for, and often excused my husband – but what's the point in writing a lie? I've been living one for long enough ...

I'd been abused for four years and nine months.

I'd recorded twenty-nine major (what I call major) incidents of physical violence (the average woman waits until approx thirty-five incidents before acting), although the psychological abuse and mind games became more and more frequent the longer we were together.

I'd not bothered to record the odd push or shove, the Chinese burns, the bites, the morning awakenings with pints of cold water or fingers rammed up my nose as a 'joke', frequent verbal abuse, frequently rejected kisses and cuddles, or looks of revulsion because time and frequency were not on my side.

I wish I could say it was the happiest day of my life. It wasn't. It was probably the worst. But it was, it is, the start of my future: one where I will not be controlled by another human being, where I have promised myself not to be a doormat, where I won't jump just because I'm told to, where I won't be in fear and terror in my own home.

Every step I have taken forward, I have been told is the most difficult one. This was the most difficult thing to do to someone you still love, in fact, would still die for, but for me as an individual it's only the beginning.

I really don't believe I've done the hardest part - that is still to come from within myself ... From memories, both good and bad, from reactions, both good and bad. From being two (in the eyes of the world) to being one, to worrying whether I'll always be one, or whether there'll be two again, to not wanting anyone except my Rob, to the fear of discovering he's staying nearby, to the jealousy and anger I feel that he can't stay here, in his own home, to the feeling of bereavement that doesn't really allow you to grieve. For the memories that I've created of my imaginary husband, the one I always thought Rob would become, to the sudden remembrance of a thump that brings me back into the reality of the violence. To the numbness that stops me remembering anything that's happened, to the insecurity of friendships, of the fear of being let down (if my own husband can do it, then how can I believe what anyone else says?), to the peace of a good night's sleep free from panic attacks, to the guilt the next morning when I think of my husband forced to live at home each weekend with parents who I like to blame. From the enjoyment of not having to look over my shoulder and jump at every noise (except I still do), to the guilt of going into every room of what is now my house, and remembering that it was Rob who made this, that or the other and made it the lovely house it is. To the indignation I feel when I find others are accommodating him and therefore putting me at risk, to the guilt I then feel because they have never known the full truth. From the happiness and liveliness I feel one day, to the depths I plunge to the next. From the fear of overburdening friends, to the recognition that I am worthy of support … I could go on … the list will never end … but for now, I'm just (sort of) thankful it has begun.

Chapter Three

21st March 2001

On the weekend of the 17th to the 19th March 2001, I felt particularly uncomfortable. I kept jumping and flinching because I could feel the tension welling up inside Rob, and I knew it wouldn't be long before he hurt me again.

However, so far as my injunction was concerned, nothing was further from my mind than the phone call I received at 8.45 on Monday the 20th March. It was an answering machine message on my mobile asking me to call Rob, who sounded really down. My first thought was that his grandma had died or something along those lines. I wouldn't usually have called him back but he sounded so bad that I just had to.

Little did I know it was to be my last conversation with him. God knew I couldn't have coped any other way. How do you say goodbye to the man you love one morning, knowing that you are about to get an injunction to stop him coming home ever again? I had always prayed that if it had to happen then it would happen this way, without calculation, although when I first picked up the phone that morning, I still didn't know what the future would hold. I try to remember now what he was wearing that morning when I peered out of the window to see if he had gone and it was safe to get in the shower. I always ended up turfed out of bed and in a different room, so could get half ready for work without him even knowing I was awake. I think it was his light blue shirt – the one we had chosen together from the catalogue earlier that month. He had his lunchbox under his arm – the lunch I'd made him – in fact, he must still have the box somewhere. It's funny the little details which come to mind, the trivia amongst the hugely important facts.

He told me that he had gone into work and they basically told him to pack his bags and leave. He had already had difficulties within the team, and had been given a month's trial at which he had succeeded, but as soon as the pressure was off and things were back to normal he had slipped back into the interpersonal difficulties that have ruled his career, and his life. I don't know where it came from, but when he said he was going up to see his parents for a few days I said that maybe this was a sign that it was time to change a lot of things in his life. He immediately asked, 'Do you mean us?' And I said, 'Yes, I do actually.' He replied that whatever was going to happen should happen amicably, and I replied that yes, this was what I wanted too, but he must not forget that I was still terrified of him. For some reason he asked me if I'd been talking to his mum or anybody, and the words just slipped out, 'No, I've been talking to Sharon.' Sharon is Robert's ex-wife whom I tracked down six months ago. He wasn't angry, but suggested we met up at lunchtime. Suddenly I knew that this was it. I couldn't go home (although I did rush home whilst I knew he was still miles away, grabbed the bag I always had packed, plus house and financial paperwork, and literally threw the cats into the cattery) and I couldn't meet Robert again because of his threats about Sharon. He had said if I ever so much as mentioned her name again he would not be responsible for what he did to me. Seeing how much he hurt me without threatening first, I dreaded what he would do if I broke a rule he'd made. Plus, this threat was just for mentioning her, he definitely didn't know before that I'd been talking to her for months. I didn't mean the words to come out yet they did, and I knew they were prompted by God, rather than carelessness.

I knew then that I would never see my husband as my husband again, and I was the most heartbroken and devastated that I had ever been in my life. I think that Rob knew that changes were afoot, but, although what he has done to me and Sharon is criminal, at that moment I loved him as I have never ever, and will never ever, love anyone else again.

I immediately got an ex parte injunction, which means one that the judge granted in Rob's absence, so serious did he consider the risk to my life. I have not felt it necessary or wise to note that many or that serious incidents in this book, but suffice it to say that no one, except God, has been there with me, and knows how I have felt, as though I have been to the edge of hell and back so very many times.

I didn't realise until later just how unusual it is to get an immediate ex parte injunction nor how seriously it is taken. When I spoke to a magistrate at a later date, she said that in court there are only two occasions in which the words ' so seriously' are used – and these are when sentencing somebody, or when granting an ex parte injunction. This was made a full injunction at a court hearing one week later, and it runs for four months, and has the power of arrest attached. The police immediately changed all my locks, added some bolts of their own, put me on a direct line to the station, stuck shock alarms on all my doors and gave me a siren.

What seemed so strange to me at the time was that the whole world carried on as normal around me. I saw neighbours taking their children to school, the postman came, the dustbin men wondered why I hadn't put my rubbish out, and it seemed irrelevant that there was no milk in the fridge. I couldn't believe that this was happening to me and the world had not come to a stop. It was like a dream, or rather, a nightmare.

I've decided that there must be an unwritten law in this country about grief. You are allowed to be in shock for a week, denial for a week, and then grieve 'properly' (whatever properly is) for two, maybe three weeks, even a few months if you're lucky. But when it goes on, when the flashbacks are worse after a year than they were after six weeks, people just give up. I have heard people make comments about bereaved people, 'Oh, is it still that that's upsetting her? But he/she died a year ago.' Grief is a personal thing. And if you've been traumatised enough then you have to face the possibility that some of the symptoms may stay with you for life – it's just that with help, it means that you rule it, it doesn't rule you.

I haven't seen Rob for nearly seven months yet I still expect him to walk through the door most evenings. When I am fortunate enough to have visitors – (several of them seem to have disappeared) – I find myself getting out enough crockery for him too. I don't really bother eating when I'm on my own; there seems little point. In fact, I don't do many of the things that used to bring me enjoyment anymore. Writing birthday cards, or any type of card for that matter, is one of the hardest things. At Christmas I didn't send any – it was simply too painful writing 'love from Vicky' when it should be 'Vicky and'.

My marriage is dead but there's no funeral. There is no communal gathering of people who love us/me/him/whoever to mourn his 'disappearance'. There is no one to share the few good, let alone the bad memories, with. It is as if our marriage was just extinguished, even though I am not even divorced. My daily reality is made up of things that seem impossible, the things that only nightmares are made of. Emotions can come upon me like a tsunami, completely engulfing; chasms of black without chinks of hope.

It was my choice, yet at the same time it wasn't – one day I was married, the next I was single. One day I took out an injunction, just to keep me safe, the next day my husband wanted a divorce, wanted me to divorce him, and, as always, I want to do what he wants.

I still couldn't understand how church services were continuing, how Sunday school children were still there, expecting the same bouncy me to materialise, how the reports still had to be written for school, how County

Hall were 'expecting' me to be back at work. How could 'normality' still exist in the middle of a world that doesn't make sense?

'Stop the world, I want to get off' is a phrase that springs to mind.

The phrase 'it takes two to tango' makes me laugh now. It might take two to make a marriage, but it only takes one person, one abusive action, to break it. Despite reiterations from many people, it's taken a long time, coupled with shame, guilt, and humiliation for me to realise that Rob broke those marriage vows the first time he laid a hand on me.

What made it worse is that we, or rather I, as if he would really take notice of these and therefore stop his abusive behaviour, chose some lovely, quite different vows. I remember us promising before God to have a marriage where the Holy Spirit was honoured, not grieved or restricted.

In the Bible, Job lost everything he owned in one fell swoop. His friends came and sat with him for seven days in silence. Perhaps they knew that he wasn't ready in his deep grief to listen or hear what they had to say. We are often critical of the advice they gave him later on, but how I would have given anything to have the presence, even the silent support, of friends at that time. I had this initially, even from the few friends that were more Rob's than mine – it's then expected a few weeks later, that you're on the road to a swift recovery – after all, the 'problem' has been removed. I guess they knew that I was not ready to hear their words, but to be joined in my silent world would have changed everything at the time. I guess they were frightened too, frightened that anything they did or said would push me over the edge. But for those readers who want to help victims of the future: we don't always need words, we certainly don't need advice so early on in our journey, but we do need to feel the physical presence of those who have always cared about us.

The fact that there were things to do and tasks to fulfil

made life so much easier those first days. It took me many months to learn that survival tactics I had learned within the violence were continuing in their opposite forms once the violence was over – the need to regain control by 'fighting' everything, everything I would once have let slip; the business in between days of sleeping and staying in bed so that time passed without me knowing ... all so that I didn't need to think. But once all the activity was over, had slowed, and the terror that filled every day had calmed to fear, I realised something – the pain was here to stay, for however long ... (and no, it doesn't disappear in a few weeks – it may become boring old news to everyone else, but when you're living with it day in, day out, night in, night out, it's not quite as easy then, is it?). People all reacted differently to my hurt. Some avoided eye contact, or 'accidentally on purpose' didn't see me, or didn't get my text message inviting them to lunch until it was 'too late'. (I couldn't use the phone for months – the fear of verbal 'rejection' was too much and I could pretend to myself that people were telling the truth – and I'm sure most of them were.) Some friends were fascinated, some horrified, many showered affection and love all over me, some said they understand (they don't). Some said they didn't understand but cared anyway. The best people gazed at me with empathy and love in their eyes with a silence that attempted to reflect back my own pain.

The best help was from people who accepted they couldn't do anything to take the pain away, but were there, to pray when I felt like it (it's amazing, incidentally, how many Christians don't feel they've 'done their job' unless they've prayed with you, even though at times I asked not to be prayed for aloud – it just was too much emotionally) and to be quiet when I didn't. Please don't pray with us when we ask not to be – just pray for us later.

I went to a self-help group for people whose relationships had ended. There are similarities between divorce and bereavement – the grieving process, the loss (which is all consuming at times), readjustment to life without a partner – I understand all of these, but what I am having to adjust to the most is the very thing that people can't understand – the change from living in danger to living in safety ... but alone, and the fact that I can still, months on, be in both love and terrified together – to be a prisoner in my home at times – just in case I see him, but desperately wanting to see him, to hug him, (not that he'd allow me to) to love him. A sudden bereavement leads to sympathy, a sudden separation with gory details of an injunction and power of arrest doesn't.

Occasionally, I feel angry with people who've been bereaved. They are treated so differently. Society understands. They go through a process, but it's different because death brings with it an automatic closure. Bereaved spouses are treated with honour where I only feel shame and guilt. Bereaved spouses can eventually celebrate and remember the good times they had together – no one wants to talk about Rob, or even about the few times when we had fun together, safe in the company of our friends. I somehow make it awkward for my friends to have a social life if I'm there.

I imagine people wondering 'Was Rob provoked?' Fortunately for me, his behaviour was such towards me in public that I know I worry unnecessarily about this. I know I treated Rob like my prince. But now he has gone, I'm the one who's fallen apart. He hasn't. It's his pride and materialism that have been dented, but the 'grief' starts and stops there. Even though the actions were my own, it's me who's suffering from depression; who doesn't know 'how' to live without his rules and regulations; it's me who's treating myself in the abusive way he used to; it's me who people keep lovingly needing to 'check up on'; and I can imagine, instead of talking about Rob and his violent behaviour, they may as well be talking about Vicky, his 'awkward', or even his 'unstable', wife.

No, I didn't refuse him anything, ever.

Yes, dinner was always on the table, packed lunch was always, well, nearly always in the fridge; there were always clean clothes and a clean and tidy house.

I jumped when he said jump.

I gave him money when he wanted it, although he had twice as much as me.

I was the one who asked how I could help him. He just once asked me how he could help me - after I told him the doctor had said I was depressed - and even then his advice was to get rid of the cats so that I was 'more loveable' and he felt more like helping me.

I never refused sex; I never neglected him.

I was always the one who was his constant support, through difficulties at work.

For five years I supported him through the problems he always had - in the whole five years I once, just once, asked for patience and support during an Ofsted inspection week, and yet never heard the end of it - the mickey-taking, the teasing about how important it was to me (after many weekends taken up by going through the same work problems of his, over and over again), and how it hurt me when he never asked once how the inspection had gone. He found out, because other people phoned to ask, but he never commented or congratulated - just asked me at the end of the week whether I thought I should take him out to dinner simply because we'd lived on microwave meals for the Ofsted week.

Chapter Four

Even months later, I still feel as though I'm the 'accused' and 'on trial'; I'm the one people are watching cautiously. Not doubting the abuse, but fearful of how I may react as I behave like a hostage released – initially jubilant and since then like someone stuck on a see-saw. Friends of decades are suddenly 'judges of my moods', talking as fast as possible lest there be a gap left for me to mention my life, my marriage, my husband, my shattered dreams. To a certain extent I owe them my life, but now they take that as an insult; when I make references about how they have helped me, I meet with fear and withdrawal. I am the only one who could have taken that decision and followed that path of action; no one else could do it for me, and Rob is far too precious for me to have acted purely on the advice of others – it had to be me, and only me that made these decisions which carried such finality with them.

But had friends not been there for me, had they not helped me draw up my safety plan and some of them even been part of it, had they not spent time praying and agonising with me, I may not be free today – I may be a murder statistic, and I would rather be free with shattered dreams, than have suffered another assault that could have killed me – well, sometimes. The reactions and broken promises of some make me think, sometimes, in my 'up and down' world, that I would rather live in danger and still have their friendship, than have frightened them away by following through the things we have prayed about together.

In some ways I have found it harder to understand and forgive friends who have once loved and cared, than I have

Rob himself. One thing I have learned through this is the value of face to face contact. So much that is written down can be misinterpreted in such emotive circumstances. But I have not wanted to upset people with my tears at the other end of a phone, I have not wanted them to hear my sorrow; I have tried to protect them, and in so doing, made things more difficult for them. It's just another way of recognising that people don't understand, that I couldn't make phone calls or initiate contact; life was far too fragile - the risk of rejection and the increased feelings of worthlessness made contact impossible by any other route.

People can't and don't understand the fear - it's probably the most difficult aspect to understand if you've not been in it. Simple things like peering through blinds to see who's at the door on a dark night, or minds working overtime when I'm out of mobile reception and don't answer can be misconstrued and make those who care angry, hurt, fearful and confused. It's not their fault, but it does add to our guilt - false guilt.

Please understand us. Please understand us more and more as you read about the trap of charm and control that you see unravelling as we travel together. There are no individuals deliberately pinpointed in my story, no particular individuals to whom I am referring, since none of my friends know how much and what other people knew either then or now. But if this strikes you (as either a personal friend or someone else whom you know has suffered similarly) with a sense of guilt, don't lose heart or feel angry, but be thankful that you couldn't understand, and honoured that you have the opportunity of helping others in the future in a more informed way. But please don't run away, and if you have to, please explain why, especially if you've promised to stand by us.

It is especially hard when people tell you that you must have had your share of 'fair weather friends' because those who spring to mind are the last anyone would label as such. But no one has given me reasons - I have even apologised in case my own depression has upset them – what more can I do? It's another waiting game – I liken it to waiting for the next assault – if those minorities had told me that our friendship was over it would be distressing but I could accept it, but when I think of those lovely promises, the ones I had to destroy in case Rob found them, it still makes me cry myself to sleep, months and months on. I have to be honest and say that within my own peer group, I can rely totally on my friends who do not claim to be Christians not to let me down, and who try and try and try again, to encourage me to socialise when I struggle with the avoidance strategies that are part of post-traumatic stress. We are called to be peace makers, and I've developed a different view of who I may be meeting in heaven one day. But I also have to admit that they don't spend every evening, every weekend socialising with Rob, like many of the others did.

None of us know who God may send to cross our paths, and if my suffering can help other people, then each step of it can be used by me, by you, by God. So for all of us who have at sometime in our lives let down a loved one, instead of putting this book down and going on a totally unnecessary guilt trip, praise God for the ways in which He could use you, should you be open to Him, in the future, maybe for those who haven't even started their journey yet, and who can't face it unless they know friends will stick to their words. I have been fortunate – had I known the pain that would be caused by friends 'running away' (or equally as a loving friend, known what I would put them through) I may not have gone ahead, and then may not be here to tell my story. But it has made my life a lot harder because I initially lost so much that I was promised I would keep. That's much of the inspiration behind this book – we need to be educated because, for one in four women, education makes freedom more attainable, more realistic and much safer.

How I wish I could have been like Job, who said immediately after losing everything, "The Lord gave, and the

Lord has taken away, may the name of the Lord be praised." (Holy Bible, Job 1 v 21 NIV) I found, five years later, a prayer I had written four days before I moved into our house, our marital home, just me and Rob. Finding it and reading it still sends shivers down my spine. I can just about remember writing it now, and I remember the feelings of fear, despair and hopelessness, but I also remember excitement, love and dreams of an exciting future. It certainly never crossed my mind (consciously) that I was being abused, even though from this day forward, my record of assaults also begins. It was a New Year's prayer written in the year 1998, and it contains many things that I now see as warning signs and signs that I must, even back then, have been in sub-conscious denial.

However, part of my prayer says:

> "Lord, take away all I have materially, let me have you, and love, if that is your desire. Help me never forget my roots – those of poverty yet filled with a love that was totally self-sacrificial. Let me have time to study your word and your world. Do what you will with my dystonia, Lord, so long as I can go on giving to others. But Lord, should you choose to improve it, never let me forget the pain and frustration of living in a body that won't do what I want it to, so that I can help others. Please use our house, and above all I pray that you will use it when it's lacking in visitors so that you can use it, without facade, when it's full. Lord, may this be a year of beginnings, not of ends. May I find myself this time next year an emotionally healed rather than further broken person, and as you were as a sheep before its shearers, help me to be quiet in the face of suffering and violence. I beg you most of all, Lord, that history will not repeat itself and hurt the one I love the most, not so much for me, Lord, but for him. But I pray that you will allow me to say with Job, Lord, 'Naked I came from my mothers womb, naked

I shall depart; the Lord gave, and the Lord has taken away, may the name of the Lord be praised.'"

I have to admit I'm not usually so 'holy' and I know that I was begging God not just for the abuse to stop, but for me to be able to keep quiet about it. When God doesn't appear to answer our prayers in the way we want, there is always a reason, and for me that reason was disclosure, not secrecy.

Little did I know just how much suffering and violence lay in store.

Chapter Five

There were times after the injunction when I couldn't really read, and I certainly couldn't pray, but we have a God who understands, and it's a good job He doesn't get bored of the 'help me' prayers that constantly shoot up to heaven!

Some sceptics say that Christianity is a crutch. This has always insulted me. But not now! If you've sprained your leg badly, then the only way to get about safely is by using a crutch. If you don't, you will be flat on your face. God, however, is big enough and strong enough to take the strain – to take the gory details friends can't cope with knowing. He is strong enough to take my desperate, irrational actions; He is strong enough to take my emotions and repetitions that are too much for others; He is strong enough to cling to when there is no one else who can understand, however hard they try.

It is true to say that my emotions can rush out like a tidal wave, completely engulfing me with despair. I try to be angry; even today the anger is almost completely self-directed rather than towards Rob. I am still waiting for the anger that I have been told will arrive quite suddenly when I'm not necessarily expecting it. I am frightened that when it comes it will never stop. That's because healing is like a scab. On a good day, when I boast that I'm better and I am making progress on my journey, that is true; it still only takes a small and unexpected incident, one that I wouldn't usually even notice, to precipitate the tears that now flow so easily and painfully, exposing the wound, picking away at the scab. The scar will always be there, but one day it will be just that – a scar that reminds me of trauma but no longer hurts, can no longer be reopened, is just a memory. But right now the changeover of emotions is just so exhausting.

But it was my decision, and I have never doubted that it was the right one. God gives us free will and choices. Without free will there can be no true love. However, I still carry a lot of false guilt, which I can now say is not mine, and I don't have to carry it. But I still wonder, and I still question, have I let myself down? Have I let Rob down? Have I let society down by becoming a one in three statistic of failed marriages? Have I let Christians down? Have I let God down?

Real guilt is healthy because it means we can seek and receive forgiveness. I feel guilt for the way in which I have spoken to people and expected so much of them. I think anyone who knows about domestic violence would say I'm being too hard on myself – I was deeply depressed, and the fact is not everyone was there for me initially like they promised, some people disappeared with no explanation – I could go on. I have asked friends for forgiveness when I think I have overburdened them, or phrased things disrespectfully. I don't think anyone actually said in a way that felt truthful, 'That's okay, Vicky, we understand,' or, 'We are sorry that we couldn't be there like we promised, but here are the reasons why.'

I found a printout of one of very many e-mails sent to the dear patient leaders of my church the other day. It was written several months before I took out the injunction. I had written it when Rob had been away for ten days and I had had some time to rediscover the real me. Instead of enjoying the fact that I was happy, I was confused and upset, and questioning God, in something as close to anger as I then knew it, as to why I had to feel so happy and bubbly when Rob was away and so frightened and timid when I knew he was returning. I am not one of these 'God told me this' type of Christians, but I was so incredibly aware of God saying to me, 'Vicky, this is the person I created you to be.' It was then also that I also felt that God wanted me to write down my experiences to share with you, and as I was driving along later, thinking and praying over God's words, I heard on my CD that familiar song 'In Christ Alone'. I knew again that I couldn't face the future on my own, or even just with my friends and family, or even with a specialist service, although they have all played a part at different times and in different ways, but I knew that it would only be in Christ, in Christ alone, that I would be able to face what I knew would be tougher and more dangerous times ahead. I had also written: "*I am not naive enough to try and pretend that this happiness is what a single life would be like all the time – I am trying also to think of the 'ripple' effects, many unpleasant, I'm sure* (Little did I know just how unpleasant) *that temporary (or permanent) separation would bring. For some months I feel I have been attempting to ignore the niggle inside that makes me feel, like my GP put it, that I am 'colluding' with the abuse by allowing it to go on, because that is what I'm doing by tolerating it. I find it most difficult of all that Rob can't understand how much I wrestle with everything that is going on and how much I'm loving and over-protecting him, and how that this love is preventing him also from being the person God made him to be. Rather, he sees it as betrayal and a lack of love. I hope he can understand how much I love him and would go to any lengths, maybe now extreme ones, in order to help him.*"

However, many people prayed and prayed. Many people I know continue to pray. Some prayed when they couldn't face visiting. So why didn't God, the king of the whole universe, actually do something? Do something to make life easier, to ease the pain, to skip out the middle, most painful part of the journey, and take me straight to survival? That sounds irreverent, but seeing as God knows what I'm thinking anyway, I may as well be honest about it. God has promised to be with me always, and I know that He has been with me every step of my journey so far, my dangerous journey and my painful journey, both as a victim and survivor. God doesn't promise anywhere to protect us from pain and suffering, but He does promise not to leave us alone in it and that He will be with us, be with me on the whole of my journey from victim to survivor, for it is in Christ alone, with Him by my side, that I can face the future.

Chapter Six

I first met Robert in 1993 although he was, at that time, an infrequent visitor to the area, just popping down for the odd weekend every now and again. I didn't get to know him at that time, but I was immediately struck by his friendliness and charm – he was the type of man you could introduce to the fussiest of parents, and impress.

It's a small world, and later on it was partly this that made me feel God must have bought this about for a purpose. A good friend of mine had gone waterskiing off a Greek island where Robert had also been at the same time. They discovered that back here in England they lived only 150 miles apart so they occasionally visited each other. I remember being surprised when my friend told me Robert was married; I wondered why he had never bought his wife down with him.

Over the next two years Robert's weekend trips to Devon became more frequent and we understood that he was having marriage difficulties. This surprised me, and, whilst I can't say I stopped to analyse it much, I thought she must be mad for not counting herself lucky – he was just so charming! Eventually Robert came down every weekend and I remember the thing that pleased me most was that he started to come to church with us and show an interest in spiritual things.

I should explain our situation at the time. Our social life was very much that of a student lifestyle, revolving around one house where about ten of us used to regularly congregate. We were all so close that we would walk in unannounced at any time, even if the house was empty, cook ourselves a meal, go for a quick snooze on someone's bed or attempt to clean the kitchen of a house inhabited by three men! We were an inseparable group during those few years. I spent more time there than I did in my tiny first-time buyer's house, purchased in 1992. It was a great social life, made even more attractive by my long-term intentions on one particular member of the household. This also meant that as time went by, and Robert spent every weekend at the house, I got to see him more too!

I don't have that many memories of him, I was so besotted with a certain other man, but as this man developed other relationships, Robert became a more focal part of our group. I remember him as excellent at small talk, quite entertaining at times, and still ultra polite and charming, but I do remember feeling that although I really knew him, I really didn't at the same time, as I'd never really had a deep and meaningful conversation with him, nor seen him chat at this level with anyone else.

In 1995 a group of six of us went on holiday to Scotland. Robert was waiting for his decree absolute by now, but seemed to be coping okay as he had found a new love in his life. (She only lasted a few months because she had a horse and he felt this took too much time away from him and that she was 'too besotted' with it.) We had a good holiday; at this time I was walking for up to an hour, but no more, and Robert was as accommodating as my other friends in thinking of my needs.

We had a few arguments on that holiday - or rather Robert did - but then a couple of the girls also fell out with each other, so I shouldn't maybe make too harsh a judgement on this.

The best thing of all was a memorable day on June 1st 1995, when one of my best friends was baptised and Robert made a Christian commitment, both at the same service. I remember singing 'There is a Redeemer' and how that hymn played a part in what I hoped naively would be the restoration of our marriage just a few years later.

In early 1996, when it was becoming obvious that nothing serious was going to happen with the chap I was so besotted with, I felt the first 'click' of interest towards Robert. He seemed so stable, so sensible, so decisive and in control of his life and those around him. I fought my feelings for a while – they weren't that strong, for some reason I could 'take him or leave him' rather than feeling that overwhelming hormone surge that I usually felt! Nothing happened and my feelings stayed the same – I wasn't particularly bothered one way or the other.

Four of us decided to do on a cheap holiday to the Norfolk Broads the following summer. The two lads had plenty of money to spare (Robert, simply because he was living back at home with his parents).

They had also already had a luxury holiday to Thailand a few weeks earlier.

A missionary friend came with us – she had had an extraordinarily difficult few years. She had been with a mission in Africa, and had had to flee, leaving all her possessions. She had seen horrific things, including the torture and death of her friends. A couple of months after her escape home to Devon, her mum collapsed and died without warning.

The holiday fell on the six month anniversary of her mum's death and she was quite quiet at times as she reflected on this. Robert was moody all week and constantly making references to her being selfish as by being quiet she was spoiling things for him. Eventually he could stand it no longer. We were out walking late one evening and Robert and she marched off ahead of us. From the large gap between us I could hear raised voices and see Robert's feet going faster and faster until my friend was running to catch up with him.

When we got back to our house, Robert was happily in the kitchen making himself a drink, as cool and calm as anything, and eventually I found the poor girl, still young, still grieving, still hurting, hidden and shaking in a tiny walled garden round the back of the house. She wanted to talk/cry for a couple of hours about what had gone on in the last twenty minutes, which initially I thought was a reaction to the death of her mum. At first I was concerned that she needed medical help as she seemed so depressed and upset and was trembling from top to toe as if she was in shock, yet I found this strange because Robert was so cool, calm and collected as though nothing had happened. I had known her for five years and had never seen her in such a state. She reported how Robert had shouted more loudly than she'd ever heard before, told her how selfish she was, that she wasn't thinking of how she was affecting him and that she should start behaving appropriately. Something inside me was very confused. I knew that she wouldn't lie, and I didn't think she was the sort to exaggerate, but her physical state did appear out of proportion to a 'normal argument'.

I remember her words: 'Vicky, my mum collapsed and died suddenly, I've seen my best friends tortured and killed in front of my very eyes, but I have never ever been screamed at in a way which makes me feel so worthless and like this.' We chatted for hours until she was worn out with tears. We waited until Robert was in the loo, then she crept inside and shut herself away in our room.

I then did something I have never done in my life before – I challenged, and challenged big time! Our other friend had also gone to bed and just as Robert was walking up the stairs to go to bed, I called him back. I told him that I felt he had been very unfair and cruel to our friend and that it was very insensitive and inappropriate of him. He kept on using the same phrases about how selfish she was being etc. (and in retrospect, many years on, I realise he never did grasp the point).

Anyhow, he listened and he appreciated my comments. At that moment I felt that sudden 'butterflies in the stomach feeling' you get when you know that you really really want a bit more out of a relationship than what you currently have. I realised that I did like him in that extra special way and that he was worth me plucking up my courage to stand up to him! I wasn't at all scared – he was charming the socks off me, and anything else if I'd let him!

Next morning Rob and I sat outside for two hours. In retrospect, this is the longest and closest to 'normal' conversation we have ever had! He told me about Sharon, his ex-wife, and how she refused to resolve issues and just blanked him when he tried to sort issues out (poor guy, I thought), how she wasn't good at compromising, conceding or negotiating and how that made him frustrated. I have to admit I can't remember the rest of the conversation, but I knew that the 'click' I had felt the previous night had just happened to him too!

I remember so clearly his words to me now: 'If I ever got married again it would be to someone just like you, because you wouldn't let me get away with the way I treat people and you would stand up to me.'

What an honest guy! I thought.

I spent the next fortnight at home, not eating, not sleeping, feeling sick, mind in turmoil (exactly like now really), because I knew that I wanted to start a relationship with him. My stomach churned as the phone rang every day and I didn't care that I was getting romantic text messages at 1 a.m.!

And so, almost five years ago today, my most precious and most destructive relationship started.

Chapter Seven

June 1998

Our first 'proper' date was on the 20th March 1996 – see, I can still remember exactly! Rob was as charming, polite and chivalrous as a man could ever be. When he went to leave he was courteous to the point of shyness so I gave him a quick kiss to precipitate him leaving and at that point we realised that we had really fallen for each other.

The next week we went to a quiet beach and spent a romantic eight hours together doing a bit of talking and a lot of kissing! I remember him telling me 'Don't always expect me to be this affectionate', but as I was having difficulty coming up for air at the time I took little notice of this!

I dared, so early on, to ask about his first wife. He told me he had encouraged her to promote her career in accountancy and she had consequently 'outgrown him'. He said he believed strongly in 'do not let the sun go down on your anger' yet she would lie in bed for hours refusing to communicate with him when he was trying to 'sort things out'. (Funny how innocent phrases like that can precipitate a flashback now – usually one of lying on the floor with size tens by my head.) He said that this, plus his lack of affection, were the reasons she divorced him, plus the fact that once he had 'held her by the shoulders to make her listen'. I often wonder today what 'holding by the shoulders' actually meant – was it a bit like 'giving me a little push to stop me having spasms?' (i.e. pushing and tipping me off the bed, screaming and throwing cold water over me, trying to push me over into a bath full of water, throwing things at me when I was on the stairs where I am extra wobbly, putting his hands round my neck?).

I tried to track Sharon down a few months before I got the injunction – I found where she lived up until June 1999 but came to a halt there. Anyway, Rob really would go berserk if he knew I'd done that. I hope for her sake she has moved, not only addresses, but from victim to survivor and I really hope she gets to read this book one day. In fact, many of the sentiments I dedicate to her, someone I'd never seen nor heard much about until I later came into contact with her.

Incidentally, long before I spoke to her, I guessed that Sharon was obviously terrified of Robert. Things were rocky at home and he knew it. He phoned her one day at work and the guy who picked up the phone didn't know who Rob was and when he asked to speak to her he said, 'No, sorry, she has the day off – she's moving out of her house today.' Apparently she was mad too! (I don't think!)

Anyhow, from March to September we only saw each other at weekends so these were exciting and passionate times, or so I felt back then. In retrospect, conversation was fairly limited and there were no love letters or silly little gifts from him to me. In fact, the little gifts and hearts and books about love which I gave him early on I've seen gradually disappear in charity bags over the last few months along with other gifts I've given him which have been things he's asked me for, and could easily have taken back, swapped, exchanged etc. I now understand this as complete rejection of me as a person and feel it reflects the lack of intimacy or understanding of sentiment. Somehow, seeing a silly but sentimental fluffy heart go out in a charity bag can cut like a knife through the feeling heart.

Going back to the early months, though, he was the absolute perfect guy to introduce to anyone. They all said, 'You've sure got a good one there,' and I believed them, but wondered why I was pleased they were convincing me that I did have a 'good one'. Had my grandparents been alive, he would have been their absolute golden boy!

I'll never forget the first time I took him to Mum's. He insisted on serving us all and on saying to Mum, 'I can't remember if you serve from the left or the right'! Afterwards he told me he thought my mum was really nice but that if she didn't have so many ornaments maybe she would meet a partner and get married again, without knowing whether she had a partner or even wanted one! He said I must tell her on his behalf because he didn't like it and it would be to her benefit in the long run.

Well, we all have our little oddities, I thought!

We had our first 'argument' in July, just four months into the relationship. (Although the day we'd ever had a proper argument would have been great because by rights an argument is two people exchanging views, negotiating, compromising and then coming to an agreed arrangement. I can honestly say that I don't remember ever once having a proper argument in our entire marriage.) Rob had stayed at Mum's and I'd already seen for pretty much the first time his notorious 'black' mood because he'd had to sleep on a sofa bed in the small spare room that he disapproved of. (His family have a huge house and loads of grounds - mine has a small house bursting at the seams with love.)

He was also miffed because my mum also has cats and they were on the beds etc. as they were in my house. Looking back, I was taken in right then by a mixture of charm, fear, love and a desire to do right; no listening, no negotiation (and although there was some compromise at the end, it was still dwelt on and brought up regularly as a major bone of contention throughout our marriage). Incidentally, the cats suffered from domestic violence too - this may sound funny, but it is actually quite normal for an abuser to also abuse family pets almost as intimidation - 'I could do this to you next ...'

Real control started here. I could have so easily finished it there and then because although he was only on the phone I remember being scared of him even at a distance and feeling relieved that he wasn't there in the flesh. Robert grew up on a farm and holds strictly to the belief that animals shouldn't live in houses. Everyone's entitled to their opinion ... but opinions don't need to lead to abuse.

Nevertheless, he phoned me from work one Saturday after we had stayed at my mum's and said that if we were ever to have a future together the cats would have to go. My initial reaction was 'no way' - at that point I didn't realise I wasn't allowed opinions or rights but learned within the next four hours of him ranting, raving and screaming, putting the phone down on me then ringing back.

'I shouldn't have kept picking it up - he was 100 miles away from me' - that's a classic example of how slowly and cleverly domestic violence starts, so subtly that you're sucked in before you realise it. I remember how shocked I was to see how averse he was to any form of negotiation, how black and white his views, how rigid and inflexible his thought patterns, and how he was unable to give me any reason why I should give my cats away except, 'You've got me now, why do you need them?'

This bizarre conversation about two pathetic but loved little cats went on for four hours! All the time he was threatening me, playing guilt trips on me, and generally disrespecting anything I said. All the time he was repeating the same phrases, phrases I was to hear literally hundreds of times over the next years like 'I don't have to justify my reasons' (yes, you do actually, I can see that now I'm starting to survive). Each time he slammed the phone down he would ring back in a charming manner to woo me, then start all over again.

Years later, after the worst attacks he would ring me on his way to work, initially to 'see if I was okay'. Once, I'd said the required 'yes' he would be verbally abusive. Only writing this now do I realise he was checking up to see if I was still at home, or had left him, or called the police.

If you are not an abused woman reading this, you will no doubt think that at this point and many others, I am weak and could have prevented much of what I've been through.

Let me assure you it isn't true. You will only understand if you've been there ...

The whole point about domestic violence is that it's a clever cycle of power and control. Once you are in submission in whatever area, there is usually extra charm and love lavished on you, often with flowers, chocolates and promises that it won't happen again. Then, once you are thinking how lucky you are to be married to someone so lovely, the next incident happens. And so it continues. You can promise yourself each time that it will be the last - that next time you will leave, but after an attack you need all your resources and inner strength just to survive. The irony of domestic violence is that really the only safe time to leave is the very time you can see no point in leaving - during the charm phase.

Anyway, to question why a woman stays is to again put the blame on her. Don't forget that Robert, in my case, was Mr Charm; it was he who was in control and me who was trapped in the cycle. And I didn't, still don't, want to be without Rob, like most women I just want the bad times to stop forever. My experiences and most books and articles on domestic mention the three phases of abuse, with which I can certainly empathise. First of all, and in my case all the time, I felt like I was 'walking on eggshells'. This would typically get worse and worse - the 'tension building phase' as its known. Sometimes, and I was never brave enough, I felt like doing something deliberately wrong because you know it's coming and waiting to see what abuse will happen is almost worse that the abuse itself. Eventually, after the assault, it's as though calm descends - men often show remorse, give partners presents, promise it won't happen again and show so much affection it's almost impossible to believe anything happened. But, as time goes on and you are trapped more and more, maybe by finances, loyalty or lack of knowledge about your options, the charm isn't needed as much. Sometimes cycles can go in weeks, even months; sometimes the cycle repeats itself several times in one day.

Rob had a spell over me. It continues to this day – it didn't leave me when he did, and sometimes I think it will remain with me forever, maybe even when he's on victim number three – and there will be a third victim, unless I'm brave enough to take action to try and break the cycle … but that's a whole new story …

I've never had a temper. I've got plenty of faults, but having a temper is not one of them. However, should anyone ever tell me, 'I wouldn't allow myself to be treated like that more than once – I'd be out', then I really don't know how I would react!

I have been a strong person in other aspects of my life: I've achieved in my working life against all the odds, I've met people with dystonia in one arm who are sitting back and collecting benefits and unable to work. My whole body is affected. As I write I have spasms that are causing constant hiccoughs and a burning indigestion. I have recently stopped typing much and rely on a speech output device. My legs are tucked up underneath me, they don't want to straighten today so I can't move far, hence the opportunity to write.

I am also managing to write this with a body filled up with opiates and benzodiazepenes. I am a fighter. I have fought each step of the way to get on a teacher training course, to pass medicals, to stay in employment, to set up my own business in preparation for the fact that the classroom may all become too much one day. I am a fighter. This must mean I can be a survivor too.

Robert did semi-negotiate up to a point, but it took four hours and continued to cause me grief and abuse throughout my marriage. It is the only point on which I have refused to back down completely. We agreed at the end of the four hours that if ever we became a permanent item, then the cats would not be allowed beyond the kitchen. I thought that he would soon budge on this one too (how ignorant I was!).

Robert has told me many times that I'd be a more loveable person or that he'd love me more without my cats. At many points I even considered giving them away. Fortunately a close friend said to me, 'Will he stop 'erupting', will he stop having problems at work, will he learn to negotiate, will he accept your dystonia, will he have a personality change if you get rid of your cats?'

I'm thankful for that friend because she made me realise that this was an issue of control and the cats themselves had nothing to do with it. Much as I'm attached to my cats, if I really thought Rob would be a different person if I got rid of them, or that the abuse would stop, then I'd have done it for him – at least, I would have done back then. Instead, as time went on and I came in from work calling 'hello', the only answer I received was a 'meow' from two frightened cats, locked in their kitchen prisons.

Chapter Eight

In September 1996 Rob found a new job as senior accountant down where I lived (I never really thought he was different from most of the others but he liked to think so) and he moved in with a chap from church who was a good mutual friend and had a spare room. He came home from work to me each night and left at bedtime.

I remember the first evening he came in from work. I was cooking dinner. I said, 'Where's my kiss?' and he replied, 'Well, I see you every day now, we don't need to be soppy anymore.' Again, I blame myself. Anyone in my situation will know how easy it is to take responsibility for another person's behaviours as though we can change who they are and how they behave. This is 'victim talk'.

When I saw Robert every day I realised how frequently little things would spark off one of what his parents 'affectionately' called a 'black mood'. For example, me wanting an early night, or wanting to watch a TV programme would start off an uncomfortable chill (he is in charge of the remote control and has been from the time we had our house). In retrospect, he was usually in charge in my own house but got in a mood on the occasions I wanted to watch something. Other 'misdemeanours' precipitating 'the mood' included him trying to ring me and me being engaged, the cat sitting on my bed, me not giving him the 'right answer' to some of the questions he was asking me about work (he had interpersonal problems there from day one). He would frequently walk out of my flat, slamming the door behind him and revving off up the road, only to ring later and be exceptionally charming and apologetic.

At the time I thought it was bad to walk away from an 'argument', now I wish he would do this rather than taking it out on me again, but of course, he would never walk away from his own house, because it would be against his 'rights'. Although I can see through the charm now, I am also aware that back then it kept me safe. It also kept me in the dark until it was too late.

I remember the first time Robert really erupted at me and also hurt me. It was soon after he moved down here. He wanted to show me his office in a village nearby. My legs were in a bad phase at the time and, as I often do, I put them up on the dashboard. Unfortunately for me, my shoes were dusty (not dirty) and he screamed like I've never heard before, not even on TV (his veins were all standing out on his head and he looked wild like he wanted to kill me), 'Put your legs down.'

I was very shocked (it came out of nowhere, no 'warming up period'), and put them down straight away … except my straight away isn't as quick as anyone else's. He screamed again and this time thumped them down with his fist. I remember being almost in shock. This seems really pathetic to me now: that sort of thing was to become almost a daily occurrence – not even worth documenting, becoming like water off a duck's back.

I cried silently all the way to his office but he reacted like it hadn't happened and paid no attention to the fact I was upset. By the time we got there I was hysterical and shaking, more because of his lack of reaction to my emotions than the punch itself. I remember all I wanted was a hug from him. If someone had suggested to me he was wrong and offered me their shoulder to cry on, I would have snapped at them and rejected their offer. Eventually after about an hour (I guess) I went into his office there and clung to him whilst he stood motionless, like a cold, still statue, and asked him to promise that he would never do that again. He told me to pull myself together and stop being dramatic, although he did say he would try not to do it again but that he 'wasn't promising'. My mind was telling me what they say about men who hit out – it will never be 'just the once', but my Rob was an exception, and, after all, my feet were dusty, and I hadn't done what I should have done – when I looked at it properly, well, it was my fault, wasn't it?

Rob did little but complain about work from the time he got his new job. Everything was always other people's fault and he would never accept responsibility for his own behaviour. At his own admittance, he expected to be treated differently.

When he first started at the company he was promised promotions in the future but by the time he'd had his first couple of appraisals it was obvious to me it was never going to happen, although he appeared completely unaware and I stood by him, encouraging him. Each review he had an 'X' in the relationships box, although he's excellent at the practicalities of what he does.

We would regularly spend whole weekends preparing for an appraisal and it would always be the same – things that I heard at home too –'Do you care that I'm unhappy? Does anyone think how I might be feeling? I don't feel supported. I feel that so and so is interfering' (contradictions?) and very many subjective and totally unprofessional points. On better days I tried to explain that these were unhelpful points to raise if he wanted a promotion.

Eventually work suggested that he saw a psychologist as he had a serious problem with reading and giving body language and had a constant confrontational and aggressive attitude. But Rob the charmer wasn't accepting the problem was with him – no, HE had made the previous company what it was (he used to tell everyone he had 'put their name on the map'), so rather than face up to himself he got a new job – a promotion – and six months down the line we were waiting to see whether he would keep his job as he upset too many people and threw team dynamics. I often think of the phrase 'I left, but I left with me' in the context of Rob and both his jobs and his relationships. What's more – he was going to tell his senior management at the review that he would give them a couple more months to change *their* attitude to him! They said that they assumed he had had similar problems in his previous job and asked questions about his ex-wife. They have also said they don't think he treats me very well. This proves to me how low my expectations had sunk because at each work social I had thought he'd been at his best. It was the results of this review that finally led to my injunction.

Anyway, on 30th March 1997 we got engaged. I was on top of the world, even though I had to put my own ring on, and, when I asked him to propose he nudged me and said, 'Fancy getting married?' without any eye contact.

Several people, including a neurologist, explained to Rob that when I came off my drugs I might experience extreme deterioration in symptoms and did he really understand what that meant etc. etc. He said that he was prepared to come home from a day's work do all the cooking, housework, etc. even if I was at home, unable to work.

I explained to him that if he was paralysed tomorrow then I would still feel the same about him as it's the person inside that counts and that I hoped he would learn to be a more loving and giving person if I provided him with as good a role model as I possibly could. I now call this making myself a victim, but I didn't know it at the time. I thought that if I could learn from other people, then so could he.

I have learned a great deal about responsibility. We are all responsible for our own behaviour and we have to want to be responsible for any changes. No one can do it except the individual themselves. At the time of writing I still feel that I am in this relationship now because I don't want to hurt him – but I am starting to learn in both heart and mind together that *he* is responsible for his own actions and for my hurt. He is the one choosing the actions which are already pushing me away emotionally if not yet physically. I still feel potential guilt, shame, betrayal, and, yes, responsibility, but

I am learning that these are misplaced. I *cannot* be someone else's conscience.

Chapter Nine

Around Easter 1997 Rob said I should put my house on the market.

I didn't want to.

I did it straight away.

It sold immediately.

I was devastated.

It fell through.

I showed disappointment but felt elation.

It sold again.

My world fell apart through the smile on my face.

I had to sell.

I had to sell when he told me to. It wasn't my life anymore. I had to make him happy. His happiness was more important than mine, he told me. This was because he might be the sole bread winner one day.

I did all the wedding preparations myself as well as all the buying and selling.

My behaviour was 'appalling'. I was too independent. I had lived alone too long.

'Maybe you've had to do all the arrangements because I'm not enthusiastic about it,' he said.

I'm not either, I thought, but then Robert had said it was stressful moving, changing jobs, getting married etc. and I'm in love and he's always right. I don't want to be independent. I want to please him. I want to be the best wife ever.

July 1999

We moved on 5th July 1997, exactly seven months before

we were married. We had separate rooms because of our principles but had, together, (because I believed what Rob said, even if it was about me) explained to our church that I was unable to live alone and needed the loving support of a 'carer' because of the stairs, size and cost of the house etc.

From this moment on, the abuse started for real. Suddenly, but not initially all the time. I guess if abuse was there all the time from the beginning then we would never fall into the trap. It doesn't work like that - I was sucked in - slowly, deeply, surely. I might have been subtly abused before, but nothing prepared me for the way things changed the second we moved.

> The following information is taken from the Women's Aid website, www.womensaid.org.uk, and is protected by copyright to Women's Aid Federation of England (©2006 Women's Aid Federation of England).
>
> "Abusers choose to behave violently to get what they want and gain control. Their behaviour often originates from a sense of entitlement. Domestic violence against women is 'caused' by the misuse of power and control within a context of male privilege. Domestic violence is learned intentional behaviour rather the consequence of stress, individual pathology, substance use or a 'dysfunctional relationship'.
>
> Research shows that domestic violence is much more likely to happen at the point of commitment in a relationship because at that point partners, without realising it, have become so used to their men's demands, that they no longer need to use charm for their partners to find, retrospectively, that they have been 'sucked in'."

Retrospectively, it may be obvious, but retrospective is too late. I spent my life walking on eggshells.

I always got the blame for 'making' Robert lose his

temper (although I believe he was always in total control of his actions) or behaving in a certain way. One of his initial 'plans' that he knew would be particularly distressing to me was that he was 'not growing in his faith as a Christian because I was 'such a nightmare'. I was mad. I was out of my mind. He had never touched me, never shouted at me, never frightened me. I was a bit funny in the head. I shouldn't flinch when he appeared. That was going to undermine him and make him worse. When he did admit to getting angry, it was me that had caused it, he 'had' to do this, that or the other because I'd 'made' him.

I mentioned before about 'walking on eggshells'. I did it constantly, but even then it didn't stop the 'tension building' phase. I used to find this terrifying as I never knew whether the 'punishment' would come within minutes, hours, or even days. All I knew was that it would eventually happen.

This phase is often followed by threats for many people; I experienced only a few verbal threats, but things like becoming generally verbally abusive, throwing things, leaving things out as 'warning signs'- in Rob's case, the sight of tools left unused in the house and a baseball bat by the bed absolutely terrified me, especially when he was obsessive about tidiness. Not that he ever used a tool to abuse me, but it was almost as if they were kept there as if to say 'don't forget, I *could* use these'. Also, in Rob's case, this threat phase often started with opening cupboards and walking around the house, as if looking for something to criticise.

Eventually, the abuse would come, and it was almost as relief to get it over with. As soon as the 'assault' – in whatever form it came – was over, Rob would immediately calm. This is the point at which he used to 'charm' me, or say it was a usual part of getting to know each other and 'settling in' to living together 24/7. After this he would minimise, deny all responsibility or blame me. Initially Rob would be loving and even unusually affectionate after an assault to the point where they became my favourite times.

My hope that everything would settle down and be okay was reinforced by this 'kind' behaviour, convincing myself, as I did so often, that things would change forever.

> The following information is taken from the Women's Aid website, www.womensaid.org.uk, and is protected by copyright to Women's Aid Federation of England (©2006 Women's Aid Federation of England)(Dobash & Dobash 2000).
>
> "Violent men will also typically justify or ignore their behaviour by:
>
> - Minimising the violence, e.g. saying it was 'just a slap' or 'isn't that bad'.
> - Justifying the behaviour to themselves and blaming the victim.
> - Denying the violence happened or refusing to talk about it and expecting the victim to just 'move on'."

Robert's first mission was to get rid of my 'clutter'. I had 'too much stuff'. These three little words instilled (and do to this day) a fear into me, as they almost always culminated in aggression or an assault of some sort. He said I shouldn't need any reminders of my past – I had him now.

Today I realise that Rob's extreme need for order and minimalism are far more deeply rooted than an aesthetic pleasure – ornaments, pictures, and, worst of all, photos, show an intimacy and sentimentality which he cannot understand. Still today it only takes a screen saver of my niece, or a drawing from a pupil, or a notelet of a cat (not even MY cats!) to attract an explosion, not always physical of late, but torrents of verbal abuse about how pathetic I am, how besotted I am, how abnormally obsessive I am and how 'there's something wrong' with me.

Rob was my first 'serious' relationship (or so he kept telling me!), so it wasn't even as if he had anything to be jealous of, but up it all went into the loft (well, the stuff he didn't force me to put into charity bags, or sneak in when I went away overnight – I am still realising, years on, that certain things are missing; I recall retrieving them from charity bags – they must have just gone back in on the next round). We were allowed no photos up, except a large one of him, smiling, taken at his first engagement! He was most insistent that this stay up in pride of place in the lounge, watching over me even when he wasn't there in person.

He seemed genuinely blind to the fact that we both had equal wardrobe space, space on the study shelves etc. – if anything he had slightly more, but it was as if he really couldn't see it (even though it was measurable, tangible), and at times my diploma and degree went flying across the study because the files weren't lined up exactly with the shelf edge, and I was, of course, doing this to 'annoy him', especially when I had 'too much stuff' already. This, apparently, showed my 'independence'; I was too much like my 'predecessor' because I wasn't quick enough in following his instructions.

There were many incidents before we were married. I can honestly say if we didn't have the house I would have got out, but I just froze – I just didn't know what to do. In retrospect I find it amazing that I had never heard of organisations that help women suffering from domestic violence – but I just didn't know such organisations existed.

Over the years I have found there to be a major overriding irony about domestic violence. That is, whenever an assault took place, particularly physically, but also emotionally and psychologically, I had to use all my inner strength, both physical and emotional, to protect myself, to survive and to recover. At this point I always planned to escape when I'd recovered, but was too exhausted from the sheer intensity and fear of it all. Then, after a few days, when things were calmer and in the initial stages, Rob was almost charming again; I was ready and strong enough to leave, and then I felt I didn't need to, because he was being okay again, and

I kept wanting to believe that it wouldn't happen again. I even convinced myself, or nearly anyway, that he was right – nothing had happened – or else I'd provoked it by being such a bad wife.

Robert managed to blame me for all his explosions – everything was my fault. Most abused women feel guilty and ashamed. It has taken months and months before I can say to myself, 'It wasn't my fault – I wasn't to blame', but many are the times when I still blame myself when talking to other people, or feel that certain things linked to any relationship that go just slightly wrong are because I've done something to warrant it. When the phone doesn't ring with that promised call, or I have to cancel something, or don't respond to a text message quickly enough – or even worse, when I read it back and realise it could be misconstrued – when things are cancelled, people are ill, it's always my fault. I sometimes feel that I'm wearing a placard that says, 'It's my fault – I deserve it', something which I'm learning needs to be dealt with before it becomes a self-perpetuating prophecy.

Even the promotion of my outreach key worker (which meant I had to have a new worker) was 'my fault' somehow, even though the 'real' me was genuinely pleased for her. Everything everywhere that was wrong in the world boiled down to me. Even if a counselling or hydrotherapy session ended five minutes early I took it to mean that I'd done something to upset someone. That's the impact that domestic abuse has – and if you're reading this as a friend, pastor, employer or counsellor please don't underestimate the false guilt that so often prevails, because we probably won't even have the confidence or self-worth to tell you, instead we'll probably just quietly go home and dream of being dead.

But at least I now know it's true in my mind: the innocence, if I don't always feel it in my heart. Robert always told me that he had never had anyone say he was difficult or abusive before. Now I know they all have. Much as I don't like to think of them suffering as I did, and vice versa, at least Sharon and I can see that there is only one common denominator – and it's neither of us! But at the time I was genuinely unsure of myself and my own behaviour. I was constantly analysing how I could have done things differently, why it was my fault, trying to make it be my fault. Because that way I could change it and stop it happening again. I would do anything to help Robert, to stop myself from being such a 'bad wife'. At one point I went from counsellor to counsellor, desperate to find someone who would agree that I was mentally ill, or behaving wrongly as a wife, because then I would have had power to stop it, and in fact the praise of counsellors for giving so much to my marriage just made it seem more hopeless. I became more and more unsure of myself. I started to believe I was mad like he said. Still today, months after I last saw my husband, I go through phases of asking people, medical, counsellors and friends, if I'm mad! I then have to check they're not just pacifying me. It's getting better – I know I'm sane now – most of the time! Of course, this isn't helped by fact that on leaving violence behind, I then started to suffer from post-traumatic stress and therefore find it all too easy to believe that he was right, and that I am 'mad'. I've recently had a police forensic psychiatric assessment, which traumatised me terribly, but also helped me in some ways. She confirmed that I have severe post-traumatic stress and that it was caused by Rob's treatment; but more to the point, as I intrinsically know already, there is no history whatsoever of mental instability or difficulties. The fact that many of my 'scores' were twice as high as the average population with PTSD I found to be both depressing yet validating. Despite this I'm also not 'mad' now, and neither are you if this is how you feel – you are traumatised – i.e. you became so used to reacting in a certain way in the face of danger that it continues once the danger is removed. Although rumour would have it otherwise, this is why so many cases of domestic violence don't get to court, because their partners call them mad, they believe them, they therefore hide their wounds. In my case

I was the main witness and although this was never said, I felt I was unreliable because of the extreme symptoms of numbness caused by trauma. (Please always show a medical person your injuries to note, even if you have no plans to leave, because if you want to take action later, even if you're convinced you won't right now, you will need their help. If you have no proof of what you have been through and then suffer psychologically afterwards, you could therefore be seen as 'proving your abuser right'.)

Chapter Ten

Rob never told me exactly what I'd done wrong, he made me 'work it out for myself'. This was terrifying, because I never knew, and was constantly on tenterhooks, both when we were on our own and when we had visitors. The latter was the worst – sometimes I knew I had said something 'wrong' whilst visitors were here and had to wait, sometimes hours, before they left and I'd receive my 'punishment' in whatever form it took. Sometimes I knew I was 'in trouble' but had to wait, sometimes hours but sometimes days, before the eruption happened. This was more frightening and I wished he'd get it over with as soon as those visitors were out the front door. Instead, we would stand there, Rob with his hands 'affectionately' on my shoulders, waving happily: the ideal couple, until the door shut.

My greatest coping strategy was to deny. Most, if not all men who abuse, also deny the abuse. Robert could smash a glass of cold water over my head after kicking me out of bed repeatedly and then say he hadn't done it – I was imagining it. But I played along. When my GP told me I was colluding I was furious. But I was – although it was never as simple as he thought. It wasn't conscious lying – it was a coping mechanism. I still loved Robert – would give my life for him. So the best way of coping was to deny it was happening – even to myself – and I became very good at it. In fact so good that even today I minimise, like most abused women, the bad things that have happened. In fact, the longer I go without seeing Rob, the less I can remember of the bad things (which statistically far outweighed the good things), so that I can really only remember the good things, and have cleverly reinvented them in my mind so that they are much better in my imagination than they ever were in real life. And one day, when I let those pretend good memories go, then Rob will go with them, because I believe that he had potential, but all I saw was bad, pure bad, and I'm still not ready to let go yet, to close the door on the man I thought loved me; the man who maybe thought he loved me too …

I have just found a copy of a note I left for Rob, with a card, in his lunchbox at about this time. I have kindly had someone go through the archive of tapes of church services as the note I had written said that I recognised that the service that day had been especially for us. I blamed myself throughout this note, apologising for flinching and promising to try not to in the future (an impossibility of course!) and to try and not be frightened (of course, Rob told me that if he wasn't aiming to frighten me, then I was wrong to feel frightened) when he got angry and approach him as the husband I wanted him to be. I listened to this tape this last week. It was about Jesus turning the water into wine and how this was his first miracle. At the end, the speaker said that he felt that this sermon was meant especially for a couple whose marriage had grown cold, where the partnership was not one of love and equality. He pointed out that God is a God who can bring restoration to broken lives and broken marriages, reminding us that this first miracle was, after all, performed at a wedding. I think this is one of only two times that Rob and I prayed together, and the prayers were identical. The only other time was the night before we got married. I started off by praying that God would make me the wife that he intended me to be, so that Rob would be really happy. Rob prayed the same prayer too – that I would be a good wife, and that he would be really happy. I thank God that, although I can look back and see my faults, I can also thank Him that in my marriage, at least, I gave 200 per cent, and I couldn't possibly have given any more. It is sometimes good to be able to realise this, in the middle of a life that is shouting 'failure, failure, failure' at me, and where in my vulnerable mind some people, even the most wonderful people I know, are inadvertently shouting this at me too.

January 2000

We were, and continued to be, good hosts together. However, I was always tense, because I could be sure that as soon as the door shut, I would be in trouble for something, making a joke about something he considered too personal, answering the phone when we had guests (yet if I was entertaining alone and he rang I would be in major trouble for not answering it), not backing him up in discussions (I don't mean formal ones, I just mean chats), laughing at the wrong things, saying things he thought made me look stupid (whereas in actual fact, I was making people laugh with me, not at me) and other such things.

Whatever 'sin' I had committed, the anger always ended up going back to the topic of cats, and how they made me 'even more unappealing and unloveable'. This is a phrase I've heard so many times over the past four years it will take a long time before I can stop believing it. I find it difficult, to the point of tears, when I have to talk about my achievements and say positive things about myself even today, yet can happily reel off endless lists of why I feel myself to be unappealing and unloveable. On top of this I was told I was a defect and each spasm mimicked, with a 'spastic' face on top just to add to the effect and I would be told, 'If I'd known what a defect you were, I'd never have married you.' In actual fact, I was doing much better than had been predicted.

People gasp, and rightly so, when they hear that you have been physically assaulted by a partner. However, the bite marks on my finger nails have grown off the tops, the Chinese burns have gone, my body has dried out from the many pints of cold water poured all over it, the bruises and marks have gone. I still have physical reminders at almost every breath because of my extra vulnerability, but in the main, the physical does heal. But the self-esteem, the self-worth, the shame, the guilt, the awful names that still ring in my ears – they are still with me because I got so close to allowing them to swallow me up completely. I have often described myself over the past years as an empty shell that is all scooped out. I feel as though I am dying inside and that I am close to emotional death. I want to return to being the person God made me to be in His image, but these scars, these memories, these flashbacks, the way I see myself, the bits I still try not to believe but partly still do; these are the parts that take so long to heal, that make us who we are and who we will be in the future. As I write, I am so close, yet not quite close enough, and I'm too scared to go through with it anyway, to have Rob charged for ABH at an emotional as well as a physical level. This is where the greatest damage is done, the scars inside that no one can see; the results outside which are devastating and many choose not to see.

I've since learnt that there are two kinds of pain from emotional abuse: the pain of change, and the pain of never changing and staying the same. I'm also learning that the more you resist pain, the stronger it appears to become. It has to be faced head on. It's a choice. A tough one. But a choice. Like abusing is a choice.

For abusing is a choice. A handful people from church who were close to my husband and who had 'discipled' him, were convinced that he was ill. It would be so nice if God could give us all a pill to swallow to make us better. We all suffer from the effects of our society. But we don't all commit criminal offences, and we do try to recognise and deal with our failings as a rule. Abusers choose to abuse. When I feel sorry for him (which at times is practically all consuming) I have to remember he's done it before and lost a wife, and everything else, and grieved. He chose to do it again. He's not ill. If he was, he would have abused me from day one. He also couldn't have hidden it so well. He also couldn't have hurt me, answered the phone, had conversations for ten minutes completely normally, put the phone down, and carry on abusing where he left off. Why wait for the right time? Why choose parts of the body that will be covered by clothes? It's a choice.

> The following information is taken from the Women's Aid website, www.womensaid.org.uk, and is protected by copyright to Women's Aid Federation of England (©2006 Women's Aid Federation of England).
>
> "Domestic violence is about gaining control, not a lack of control. If an abuser is careful about when, where and to whom they are abusive, then they are showing sufficient awareness and knowledge about their actions to indicate they are not out of control. Who is responsible for the violence? The abuser is. Always. There is no excuse for domestic violence. The abuser has a choice to use violence for which he is responsible and for which he should be held accountable. They do not have to use violence. The victim is never responsible for the abuser's behaviour."

I am not responsible for Rob. A lovely book given to me by a dear friend from church says: "Faith is … committing a loved one's problems to God to solve … having confidence that God will take the bad choices others have made that affect me and use them for my ultimate good … seeing that I may always live with scars from healed wounds of the past, God has incorporated them into His perfect plan for my life … and trusting God's final outcome when all I'd dreamed of for my loved one is shattered." ('Faith is', Pamela Reeve)

Chapter Eleven

I lived in terror for most of those seven months before we were married. There were 'incidents' almost daily. It was at this time that something inside me told me to keep a secret diary, one that recorded many of the worst incidents. It seems bizarre and unthinkable to me now that it still never occurred to me (consciously) that I was experiencing domestic violence – I just thought I should try harder until I would eventually get it right. But every time I came close the goal posts moved – so that I would fail, be punished and be humiliated into his power and control again.

I became so used to living like this, although I still didn't really think there was anything wrong with our relationship – things like hiding the kitchen knives, or at least putting them in the dishwasher when I heard him come home, emptying a hot kettle if it had just boiled – became subconscious yet instinctive behaviours. The daily incidents were so normal that I barely noticed the things that once had made me hysterical, in fact, I used to look back at episodes like the dusty feet on the dashboard and think how stupid I was to be upset about it – I could always justify Rob's behaviour – it was a new car, it was thoughtless of me, he was right, he was tired, he had a new job, he had a wedding coming up. It never occurred to me that I had these needs too and that they were equally valid. So most of the things I have lived with have never been recorded.

Some things I remember well. Like the chocolate biscuit incident. Sounds like the title of a humorous poem, doesn't it?!

I had been shopping and filled the cupboards. Shopping

is an effort for me, so when I do a big shop, I make it worth my while. I have my own 'system' – the cupboards are basically tidy and I do all the kitchen and domestic chores and I know where to find everything.

This particular day I had bought lots of packets of biscuits. I kept these in the bottom cupboards and preferred to empty them out into a big container so when I was making Rob's packed lunch I could just reach in and pull something out, and be sure to get something different each time. This occasion he was looking in the cupboards. He made a comment about how nice the boxes would look lined up neatly in the cupboard instead of emptied out. He had his head in the cupboard at the time and I thought he was joking, so I laughed! BIG MISTAKE.

WHOOSH! All the packets and biscuits and boxes were swept out of the cupboard and thrown all over the kitchen floor whilst he screamed and shouted and swore and hovered over me holding a tray in a threatening manner. I was taken aback and scared and said that I would put them back wherever he wanted. But, as usual, by now Robert had 'lost it' and was shouting, screaming (almost as if he was crying in frustration and anger at being 'thwarted') and swearing. He started on about the cats and the 'I don't have to justify myself. If only you'd get rid of your cats you'd be more appealing' etc. etc. Then he said that he would open the doors and throw my b***** cats outside (they had never been out and would have almost inevitably got run over or lost).

I was so scared that I found myself on the floor. I can't remember the preceding seconds or how I got down there except that I was screaming 'no' (I'm not sure whether this was about the cats or something else). When I 'woke up/ came round' I felt as though I was on the ceiling, looking down at the filthy smelly body, hearing it scream, as if it didn't really belong to me. This happened quite a lot when the fear was at its most intense or the attacks were more violent.

Then I was sick everywhere. I heard that Robert had shut the outside door and saw the cats were still both inside. He looked at me, turned up his nose in disgust, told me I was a filthy animal, walked out of the room, slamming the door behind him, and left me lying in my own vomit. He was right. I was a filthy animal. I felt ashamed and disgusted that as a human being I could act so disgracefully. This image haunts me to this day despite it being a more minor incident.

Another time, Rob had had a quiet day. He didn't then, and still doesn't do 'free time' well. He is always on a hunt for excitement through holidays, parties, entertainment or shopping. I knew that a quiet weekend would be both my dream and my nightmare rolled into one.

I remember going upstairs after dinner to see him pacing around, opening and shutting doors and drawers, and looking at shelves, tutting. It's always a bad sign.

'You've got too much stuff' (Oh no, I thought). But I had a clue this time – he was in the study looking at the shelves. 'Do you really need all this?' (How dare I question him!, but yes, actually, I really needed all of it.)

'Well, no, I suppose these could go in the loft, as long as they're near the entrance where I can reach them.' He said how messy my books were. This was because they weren't all lined up exactly to the millimetre.

Now, I'm a perfectionist – at least I thought I was in the days BR (Before Robert). He had all files, all the same type, so they could be neatly lined up. I, on the other hand, had books too and they were arranged in height order but that was as good as it got.

'Your things are taking up too much space.'

'But we both have the same number of shelves.'

OOPS! I wish I could remember that I shouldn't question him. That I shouldn't give my opinion – or stand up for my right to have my own possessions etc.

My diploma and degree were pulled out again and course notes and essays went all over the floor as the shouting, swearing and screaming started. In those days I still had emotions, and I was still shocked, so I cried. This was like adding fuel to the fire, and by the time we were married I had learned that it was in my best interests not to cry – ever. Not ever. Not under any circumstances. It made me more unappealing, more unloveable, more pathetic and it certainly didn't make him want to hug or cuddle me.

It's probably three years since I cried – really cried, cried enough to let out all the hurt inside and restore my sense of balance. I'm learning to cry now – first just a little in a safe place like an outreach meeting, then at home. Initially it made me feel worse – even suicidal – now I can cry for a few minutes when something hurts, and feel better. Usually, at other times, since the post-traumatic stress has got its tight grip, it reminds me of my pupils who self-injure, smashing their heads into walls. We always have padded areas and gasp in amazement at their abilities to find the one piece of unprotected wall on which to hurt themselves. I'll never question this again. How can you get pain and frustration out and make it real if you can't feel it? How do you know you're real when the world around makes no sense.

Anyway, I cried. Robert wanted to 'discuss it'. I felt faint. 'Discussion' was always a really bad sign. I had to go to the loo. I was in there for five minutes with my head between my knees, trying to breathe deeply and stop my head spinning, my legs shaking and my heart pounding.

Robert was furious I had spent too long in the toilet – he knew it was an excuse – how dare I ignore him when he was trying to talk to me. (After that, for months I had to ask permission to go to the toilet, leave the room, answer the phone etc. without permission.) I tried to explain that I was upset because these things were important to me, but it was pointless once the rage started. He was angry that I'd been in the toilet for too long and that was that. He stormed in there looking for evidence (a phone I think) and found nothing, except my electric toothbrush which he broke in half, smashed, and threw downstairs. An aggressive act usually stopped the mood, as if smashing something or hurting me made him feel suddenly better.

Later that evening a friend came round and Robert seemed in a good mood again. I went to bed early as I was always emotionally drained after an 'episode'. Suddenly I realised I had no toothbrush so I put a new head on Robert's electric one for myself. I then swapped heads back but left the brush in the bathroom without putting it in the en suite. Rob was, at that time, sleeping in the main bedroom with the en suite (of course) whilst I slept in the spare room.

The next thing I knew it was midnight. Robert charged into my room, switched on the main light calling me a selfish b**** for not putting his toothbrush back, and pulled the duvet off, followed by the obligatory pint glass of water poured all over me. I was especially scared as all this happened in the seconds I woke from sleep. I got downstairs as fast as I could (I could almost run then in an emergency – I was still on my main drugs). I got into my car and just drove, in my nightclothes. I was heading for the back of the flats where I had previously lived.

But I only got round the corner when I felt I was too frightened to go anywhere without Rob. I wanted to go back to him. It was as if only he could save and rescue me. I found this so weird at the time and I still today have remnants of similar feelings left, even though I think I'm nearly ready to make the break.

I've read about it recently, and I think it's called the Stockholm syndrome, where hostages formed such a bond with their captors that they fled to them rather than the police when they had the opportunity. As a teacher, I can now understand why abused children would rather stay with an abusive family than be taken into care. We don't want to lose our partners, our families; we just want the abuse to stop.

I sat outside our house. I saw Rob's light go on and he phoned me in a charming manner to 'see if I was okay' (what did he think at midnight, when I was out in my pyjamas?!) I said he had frightened me, but he begged me to go back into the house. I said I would but he had to promise not to hurt me and that he would get some help the next day. He told me to 'p*** off' and put the phone down. I dozed in the car until I saw his light go off. I waited a while longer, crept back in and wedged a chair under my door handle. When I woke in the morning, I moved it in case it sparked it all off again.

After all, it was nothing really, was it? I was just being over sensitive, and, as Rob so lovingly reminded me the next day, I'd not had such a serious relationship before.

We had marriage preparation classes together with our pastor and his wife. They were obviously very skilled at what they were doing. However, I was terribly anxious about the sessions right from the start. In retrospect, I know exactly why. I knew, subconsciously, only that I needed help to get out – I couldn't go through with it, but I trusted their wisdom and felt that if they didn't pick up on anything then it was a sign I was just being silly and oversensitive and that my Rob was right.

One session was about communication. There were some poignant questions in the workbooks they had made for the sessions. I remember answering one of the questions in full on a large sheet of paper making reference of how terrified I was of Robert when he 'flipped' and 'accidentally on purpose' leaving it there at their house. Bless them, they are so good that they never even opened the booklet before we got there the next week. By this stage I had already become so confused that I thought this meant that I shouldn't make a fuss and that everything would be okay!

(I was sorting out some of Rob's things recently – I want to pack each item myself with love and care – wrapped with a kiss and a prayer even though he probably hates me now – but I'm not having some bailiff handling his possessions. I found his marriage prep booklet, and read through it – tears streaming down my face at the adoring things he had put about me. But then something struck me – it glared out at me from the page, and the feelings of 'I've failed him – he's my responsibility' all came back again as I read the page where we had to read the statements and tick yes or no. One said, 'I don't much like the person I am, and marrying my partner will help me overcome this'. Of course, Rob being Rob would not have been completely honest, but the fact that the tick was halfway between 'yes' and 'no' will live with me forever.)

Chapter Twelve

We went to Bournemouth exactly five weeks before our wedding. I remember it well, as Mum was making the bridesmaids' stuff. I went upstairs to look at the stuff and we had a conversation in passing about whether the dads would wear the same waistcoats as the ushers or different. It was only a passing conversation to which Mum innocently made reference afterwards downstairs. One of the scariest things is that, as an abused woman, you have no control over what other people so innocently say and do, which might inadvertently get you into trouble.

On the way home Rob was furious because I had 'obviously' been discussing stuff with Mum and without him. He started screaming at me louder and louder till all the veins were sticking out on his head and I thought he would spontaneously combust. He was driving on a busy dual carriageway and his driving was getting faster and more erratic and I was terrified. Although I was frightened of his mood, I was even more terrified we would crash in the central reservation and pleaded with him to slow down. He became even angrier at my suggestion as this showed apparently that I wasn't listening to him, and he slapped me hard on the thigh.

As usual, I learned after a while, once he had hurt me I would be okay physically for a while at least and he did calm, as if he needed to hurt me in order to regain control of himself.

When I got home he saw me get my camera out and take a photo of the handprint on my thigh. He told me not to be so stupid - he hadn't really hurt me, he'd only slapped me because he was 'driving and couldn't do anything else to me'.

Our wedding day was really the happiest day of my life - no two ways about it. I wasn't pretending, not even subconsciously; it really was fantastic. The day went well and smoothly, even though Rob was the only man in the church who didn't tell me I looked lovely (he said it in his speech in a very forced 'this is what I have to say' way).

We went to Algeria on honeymoon and had a great time. I was still taking a fair amount of powerful muscle relaxants and even in the heat I could walk around with frequent breaks in the heat, albeit with an odd gait. Robert got slightly moody one day when I couldn't go any further and spoilt the trip to the Sahara by saying how selfish I was because I couldn't keep up with everyone else on the sand dunes when we went for the camel rides (I was also the only one to have to have a horse and carriage as I couldn't balance), and even then, on honeymoon, he didn't wait for me but rode off into the beautiful romantic sunset on his camel with a group of strangers whilst I waited behind for them to get my pony ready.

But apart from this we had a great time - we managed to spend a whole fortnight together on our own, with no physical incidents until the second-to-last day. This came from nowhere - we were riding at night on a 'tuk-tuk' (a sort of covered bike/trailer) when we saw a clothes shop. We'd had an all inclusive package and had eaten rather well (I am still suffering three and a half years on!). I suggested that Rob would now need an XL instead of an L and called him 'fatty' affectionately, and he started pinching and twisting my arm Chinese burn style but doing it behind my back so that the other passengers couldn't see. I was sobbing, not because it hurt much but because I couldn't believe this was happening to me on my own honeymoon and I just wanted to go home and see my friends.

The rest of the honeymoon passed in a daze. The only other thing I remember was that I wanted to hold his hand when the plane was taking off as I was new to flying, but found no comfort or protection.

Chapter Thirteen

July 2001

Professionals call it dissociation. The numbness I mean. The fact that I can recall events as reliably as if it were yesterday, but I can't see or feel them happening to me. I feel now how I felt during attacks, especially the earlier or worse ones, as though I've shrunk and am sitting at the bottom of a big padded envelope just peeping out, or that I'm 'floating' on the ceiling looking down. In both cases I'm looking down at a big man attacking a smaller woman, who is me, but isn't.

I tried to find the word 'dissociation' in a book. I found it in a useful book called *It's My Life Now*. Copyright © 2000. by Meg Kennedy and Roger Hock. Reproduced by permission of Routledge/Taylor and Francis Group, LLC.

They talk about 'traumatic bonding' and if I could ever explain to someone in the following paragraphs how I feel about Rob and about me, then this is it:

> *"Traumatic bonding is a theory that tries to explain why abusive relationships are so powerful … First, for traumatic bonding to take place there must be an 'imbalance of power' …This means that one partner is much more in control of key aspects of the relationship. If your partner made most of the decisions, set himself up as the authority, intimidated you through threats or violence, or made you feel powerless in other ways, the power in your relationship was completely lopsided. The second factor is the sporadic nature of the abusive behaviour. In most abusive relationships the bad times are intermingled with the good times."* (Or in my case, less bad times.) *"The abuse is usually followed by very loving, giving periods."* (Again, not for me, but Rob

was kind in subtle ways, by letting things slip that he would usually have become abusive about.) *"This pattern of on-again, off-again abuse and affection is the strongest form of reinforcement."* (Maybe this means it will be easier for me as I never had any real intimacy or affection in my marriage, although it would not be true to say there were absolutely no happy times.)

"The third factor in traumatic bonding involves a kind of denial. You were in denial when you told yourself, "It isn't really that bad". You devised excuses to somehow make the situation better than it actually was." (Tell me about it!) *"You may have altered your attitude about the violence or found new ways of thinking that concealed the truth from yourself.*

Even beyond this, if the abuse was very severe, you may have found ways of escaping the violence as it happened by imagining you were outside of your body, looking down on the terrible scene that was occurring. This psychological defence, known as dissociation can be a powerful tool to create distance between yourself and the violence. This can be a sign of or lead to Post Traumatic Stress Disorder.

All these forms of denial and distancing are forms of what psychologists call cognitive dissonance. What was happening to you was so bad and so far outside any of your expectations of the world that it just did not fit into your sense of reality. So you relied on these techniques to try to make it fit. In order to survive, you had to change how you saw reality.

The last factor on traumatic bonding involves finding ways to mask the abuse. You may not have admitted the abuse to anyone including yourself." (I did this for nearly four years and then people wonder why I need to talk about it so much!)

"Once this bond is established, it becomes terribly difficult to break free of the relationship.

It is also likened to the bizarre relationship that is known to occur at times between hostage takers and hostages. The victim is threatened with great physical harm and perceives the perpetrator of acting out these threats. The victim sees no

> *way of escape and perceives her life depends on her captor. The victim feels isolated and holds little hope of intervention by family and friends. The victimiser offers kindness along with the violence and thus increases the victim's perception of complete helplessness and dependence on him."*

This is what it was like being married to Rob – I felt that I needed him so much I almost became him. The things I disliked about myself, I am only just realising, are not my faults (though I have many of my own) – but his. I felt, and sometimes still do – it strikes at the most strange times – that Rob is my only hope of survival and I cannot live without him. Although I know this is an unhealthy bond, I feel that it could be stronger than a bond that would have grown out of a non-abusive relationship.

I was there throughout all the assaults, yet I wasn't. This poem explains exactly how I felt and still do during flashbacks.

The Encounter

it was an encounter of the near death kind:
i left my body
i detached and looked around
saw nothing, was nothing
was safe in the beyond.
when I came back you stood over me
clenched fists, bloodied hands
back in my body I felt the hurt of your hits
my swollen face looked back at me in the mirror
sore ribs convinced me you had kicked me
i wouldn't have known; i wasn't there
while you were breaking up my body
i had left you;
it was an encounter of the near death kind.

Breaking Free From Partner Abuse, Morning Glory Press, 1993. Compiled by Mary Marecek

June 2001

How do I feel? People look at me, people who've known nothing was wrong, and they tell me how well I look and how there's something different about me. My GP said I was walking faster and my posture was different, so my dystonia must be better.

It's not. It's exactly the same. I still dislike myself, but just every now and again, when I force myself to make the effort, I feel I have the value of a snail, instead of a slug. I can sometimes look people in the eye. I'm still ashamed, but every now and again I can lift my head high and lose the shuffling that comes from the depression, not the dystonia.

When I got the full injunction for four months and when the judge insisted on the power of arrest which Robert so badly wanted removed, I was jubilant. Sad, scared, but jubilant. Rob messed around with utility bills, I had letters threatening to cut me off – I went back to work full time (immediately did four weeks in a row – more than all the last year put together). I had to work, work, work, sort, sort, sort, make one phone call after another – it didn't stop for several weeks. It kept me going. I started sleeping. I'd not slept more than two–five hours a night for several years. Now I can sleep fifteen. I suppose life passes quicker that way. The panic attacks stopped – the night-time panics literally stopped like the flick of a switch from at least one a day – sometimes lasting up to four hours at one go – to zero. Eight months have passed, and I've only had one, right at the beginning of the injunction.

There was so much to do. It stopped me thinking. I could put aside the emotional dealing - the'sorting out' I needed to do.

Suddenly, this last week, there are no letters to react to or sort, no endless strings of phone calls. I have spare time, a bit, time on my own, time to think. And, whilst I'm grateful that I'm still sleeping in the main, and I'm still having virtually no panic attacks like before, there's nothing practical to sort. Well, I am unpacking my boxes from my flat – just four years later (all my possessions have lived in the loft since moving day!), but I can think while I sort!

I don't like thinking. I've found it's dangerous. So I've become numb. I didn't choose to become numb. I have enough knowledge of psychology to know that this is dangerous. I can sit and explain the most horrific things in my outreach sessions and my voice will go shaky and my eyes will well up, but then I can cut it off. Like the flick of a switch it just goes – I don't know where. I'm not trying to be awkward, I'm not trying to make situations difficult – something hurtful just arises, and then, just as suddenly, it disappears. I try to keep with the memory, try not to divert, but have, after so many years of being told how unloveable and unappealing I am when I cry, learned that I can even carry on talking about a hurtful situation whilst 'disappearing' somewhere else. I don't know how to stop it since it's not a conscious process. I know I have to let myself hurt till I cry so much I can't stop. I'm partly writing this because I think if I make myself read it out loud then I'll cry, but when I cry I won't stop reading, not until I get to the very end.

I wish I could cry to order. I wish I could say, 'I'm seeing my keyworker later – I need a good cry,' but then I'm so pleased to be there because they are the only human beings that really understand that this immediately makes me happier. I wish I could cry when there's someone sympathetic around, but the tears will never flow then. It only takes small things – like seeing a pair of boxer shorts I accidentally-on-purpose forgot to pack up for Rob, or remembering how the kitchen blind should be pulled so it lines up with the tiles and then remembering I don't have to do that anymore – that can cause a sudden flood of tears, or attempt at it.

But today I don't think I have the guts. I might be free from Rob (for the moment – haven't a clue what will happen on 31st July 2001 11.59 p.m. when the injunction runs out) but I'm not free from myself. People are right – the physical does heal (although this week the doctor detected four healing rib fractures that are unlikely to ever fully mend as I'm always in spasm. This means I can't take deep breaths or breathe properly and I know this will cause long term health problems and that, in the true physical sense, the abuse could one day kill me). I don't know if I would have dystonia in my neck, or be falling, or be on the same strength opiate if I'd never been through all this, or if I'd be safe to take the drugs I was prescribed or use the equipment I was given, or had the house adapted. Ironically, I came off the one drug that controlled my symptoms to get pregnant. I have no baby, have irritated my husband more by my uncontrolled movements, and not been able to go back on the drug because it would seriously reduce my alertness. So I've lost everything in one go – my husband, my chance of children and my health. I've never wanted much – just a quiet, happy family life. Rob would say he'd lost too – but I don't expect he cares about me – just the house and what I consider a luxurious lifestyle. That hurts too. I was just a means to an end, an end which ended without what we went into it for.

Chapter Fourteen

I was told yesterday that I stand to gain for criminal injuries compensation, but how could I live with myself if Rob got a custodial sentence? Maybe the two don't have to link. It would be great if I knew he'd have to attend a domestic violence course, but I have little control over that once I've reported it. (Actually, later I was to find out that victims of domestic violence do actually have a say - and can ask the courts for restorative rather than punitive measures.) The money would be useful - I need adaptations - but the one big issue is that none of this, physical, custodial, financial, is anything compared to the pain of life after an emotionally, verbally and psychologically abusive relationship.

How do you live with the shame, the humiliation, the guilt, the loss of any self-worth or esteem. People wonder why I'm feeling insecure about friendships? Well, my one and only true love let me down, so why should I believe other people? It's all so straightforward to them - but they haven't been belittled, mocked, humiliated, sworn and spat at, looked at with revulsion, laughed at, had their disability 'copied' with great mockery - probably not even by strangers, let alone the most important person in their life.

I know that in the last month, and probably for many months to come I will swing between the 'real' me (who I have to remind myself is quite bubbly and humorous) and someone who worries, is unsettled, constantly on the go (or on the run!), alternately passive and determined to fight, fearful and insecure about friendships, unsure as to who to approach with what and when, thrilled with my new life, terrified of my new life, thankful when no other keys turn in the lock at 6 p.m., upset when they don't, glad that no one's mentioned Rob, upset that they don't ... The list is endless and the sad reality is that I can't expect the best friends in the world to adapt and change as quickly as my moods probably will, and I'm scared that for their own sanity they can't cope with the long haul. I hate myself for even expecting them to try.

I feel that some people think I'm dirty and unacceptable. I've just offered my home for a new six-week course the church is running - I've said that the only way I can attend at the moment - because of the physical pain and restrictions and the fear that comes with going out, away from the phone number with the history marker, the doors with the shock alarms and the telephone with direct dial to the police station - is if a group meets at my house. New venues have been chosen, but not mine, and to make matters worse, someone 'accidentally' invited Rob to a group, the group which just so happens to contain all my best friends, and puts them in an unenviable position. We have been trying to get Rob to this group for three years to no avail - but he's going now because he can abuse me this way! This has meant that my whole support network has temporarily been swept out from under my feet, and more to the point, no one else can see it - they just hope it will help him. The church congratulate themselves on advising him to stay away, for encouraging him to move away as soon as possible, whilst confusing him, and placing me in danger in the interim. If I am confused, as someone who understands some of the psychology of relationships, what is this doing to him? Condoning his actions, I would imagine. And yes, it should be clear by now that an abused woman has been made to feel so useless, that misinterpretation is quite possible, so anyone getting up in a rage at this point may as well give up any ideas of counselling or pastoral work, but it hurts just the same, accident or no accident, misinterpretation or no misinterpretation. So I've had to sit at home alone, whilst my perpetrator gets to be included in a church group of friends, which is difficult for them too. This is the toughest thing I've had to face, post injunction. If this happens to any of my friends, God forbid, then they can be certain I will *not* be sitting, reading God's word and praying with their abuser either in my house or in my friendship group. I just don't understand how anybody could believe me yet do this to me, do this to themselves, do it to Rob and further push him into denial, do this to God.

But again, I see my own confused messages in this and can blame myself as well. You see, I so badly need Rob to see Christian love and understanding in others. I think I have given many mixed messages by saying this, and even caused people to assume I would like him to be invited to groups etc. I have been praying so much that he will go to church elsewhere, and this is what he is doing, so I am really encouraged. I am fortunate that he goes away every weekend - somewhere, life for him has gone another complete circle, a bit like when he spent every weekend down here when his marriage before was on the rocks. Except this time, the game's up because we know. I hope he will find a good church, where they will look after and shepherd him and take over from where my church left off. Maybe yet God will use this situation to glorify Himself in Rob's life too.

I've always found it strange how, had I been mugged and assaulted on *one* occasion by a *stranger* in a park, I would have been 'acceptable' to friends, but when it's ongoing and caused be the person I love, yes love (I don't gloat over the fact he's lost his house, his job, his wife, his 'skivvy') it's as if I've suddenly, as the victim, lost my rights for inclusion. Think of the drama which would have been made if I'd been mugged on the streets of London!

One Sunday, a prayer was prayed by one of our many leaders, thanking God that none of us need face fear behind our own front doors. I sent a polite e-mail suggesting that this was not true and is statistically not true for up to one in four women for whom home may be the most dangerous place. I'm not just concerned with myself, my vision is that our church be open and welcoming and a haven for abused women. This was now well over a year ago. I have never received a reply or acknowledgement, and it makes me feel tainted and filthy. However busy you are, how long does it take to send one quick acknowledgement or apology to a person in crisis?

Chapter Fifteen

When I first spoke to Gill, my counsellor, she said the situation was so severe she had to break my confidence. She urged me to go to the police but I was so adamantly against it that I said I would tell them I was making it all up. So instead I asked for our minister. To this day I feel guilty expecting of him what was the job of the police, not just for his sake but for Rob's too. He met with Gill and I and was great. I remember, in those early days of 'coming out', I was terribly worried about what would happen to Rob, above all concern for myself. I asked our pastor, if we split up would the church be there for Rob as well as me? and he said 'No, not necessarily'. Ironically, because I love Rob so much that statement kept me in the relationship that bit longer yet ironically now, I fear that actually the church may go back on this. (The magistrate said to me, 'Be careful of churches - they're great places for sinners.' She's right, and it's a good thing. It wasn't really the right time to explain my beliefs to her just then, but she had a point - but one that does put me in physical danger.) I do believe in God's protection, and know with assurance that when I die, and by whatever means, I will be safe and with God for eternity. However, on this earth, right now, the physical practical things keeping me safe are my police siren, the buzzer in my home linked to the police, the shock alarms on my doors and the power of arrest attached to the injunction.

Prayer didn't stop the abuse. Prayer for Rob, not just for me. I have no question whatsoever that God could have changed Rob, that He still could, but He has currently chosen not to, and I know this must be for a reason. I thank

God that this hasn't shaken my faith in Him and I have to remember it's Him I trust in, not other believers – they are only human and will probably let me down. But then I imagine I've let them down too, by overburdening them, by telling people who already have too much on their plates, by expecting them to read my mind because I've not been allowed to express myself for so long.

At the moment, I feel like an annoying and rather pointless part of the body of the church, a bit like an appendix that has just flared up and everyone wishes would go away. This is victim talk – I know they love, support and care deeply for me, but I am scared that they can't put their actions into words by physically protecting me from my abuser. In reality, it need be such a small issue, but when you live in fear everything is magnified so much. It was the same at work when I saw a van with a company name on the side. Once you have recognised the abuse, it takes you from major assaults, no reaction, to small assaults, major reactions. I am so fortunate in my church that I can now start to see this vision turn into a reality and am so proud to belong one of only a few churches that are prepared to move into the twenty-first century with regards to unpleasant social issues.

I still need prayers – I need them to keep me safe, I need them as I have ongoing decisions to make. When you first have a crisis, people pray. When you still look miserable six weeks down the line, it starts to get boring, let alone six months! Once all the 'anniversaries' have passed, will there be anyone left who remembers I'm in pain? I've coped with his birthday, Christmas, my birthday, Easter; I have yet to deal with the next wedding anniversary, the not knowing whether the divorce will be through by then, or whether I'll officially still be married. People would think it's weird when I say I sort of hope I'm still married by then, because four years of marriage sounds so much better than three. I have possible prosecutions, compensations, and further legal challenges to settle, let alone time for me to sort out my emotional damage.

To most people, my problems will be in the past by then, unless they have suffered a huge loss or trauma themselves and therefore understand how long it takes to adjust.

When I think again of a favourite verse of mine, Jeremiah 29 v11, I pray this for Rob too: "For I know the plans I have for you, says the Lord, plans to prosper you and not to harm you, plans to give you a hope and a future." Rob may yet need to go through justice, initially causing more pain and more brokenness in order to achieve this - I don't know. But the same God who holds my future holds Rob's, and whatever sceptics may say, I believe that if God started a work in his life, and that, of course, I don't know, He will - maybe through brokenness, maybe through a prison cell, maybe through a perpetrator course, maybe through His word alone - carry that work on until completion and to heaven, where there will be no fear, no abuse, no violence, but also, none of our more unsavoury and easily hidden faults and sins.

Chapter Sixteen

April 2001

It's only eight weeks since the injunction. In many ways I can't believe how quickly I have moved on. Maybe this is part of the problem I am feeling just now. During the last couple of weeks, I have been fairly bright and bubbly, barely thinking about the past abuse and feeling full of enthusiasm about new pupils starting in my class, about ways I could redo the house and various other things. But now it's Sunday night and I feel low. I'm always so tired. I never seem to get the chance to rest at the weekend – there's always so much do and so much to sort and a social life I desperately want to pretend I'm keeping up with.

I've been in contact with the Baptist Union of Great Britain, and they do a fantastic pack on domestic violence titled rather appropriately 'It doesn't happen here'. I have said to them how wonderful and caring and supportive the church are trying to be of me and there is no way in which I could dispute this but I am so, so frustrated that I can hardly bear to think about the future because they just do not understand the fear I have of the unknown as to whether Rob will come to church or whether he will stay away. He has been advised to, but it's still 'his right', reinforced by his membership. People keep saying, 'No of course he won't', without realising this just isn't good enough for me. My intense feelings of love come and go, but I do still feel what some would say is overly sorry for him and I still feel a failure that I couldn't teach him to love and that I couldn't teach him the wonders of communication with all that entails, and I have started to feel vague sentiments of anger, something quite new to me, that no one ever cared about Robert enough to really seriously and consistently challenge him. To him, with his line of thinking, this will mean that he thinks the church condones the way he's behaved. We know that our children need boundaries if we love them, in a fair and caring way, and this is the same for the church. I've been looking at various Bible passages which back this up and I really feel that his membership should be removed not simply because he hasn't been around for a long time (which is what I'd been told might happen), but because someone is strong enough and cares about him enough to point him in the right direction and point out what he's done is wrong. As I've always managed to forgive Rob, I can, likewise, forgive the church because I realise that we are caught up in a long line of churches who no longer hold to such tight social boundaries in the same way that many parents, teachers etc. unfortunately don't nowadays. However, this pales into insignificance compared to what I was actually told by someone else in the church - believe it or not but someone actually said to me, 'We don't discuss or "discipline" people just for divorces at our church these days.' DIVORCE? What on earth has that got to do with it? What planet are you on? This has absolutely NOTHING to do with divorce - it has to do with repeated GBH and my life being in danger!

I won't pretend I don't want his membership taken away for myself as well because I do want to know that I can be in one of my most special places without him being there, but I do care what happens to him too and I still feel others putting pressure on me to do something and take responsibility for his behaviour because nobody else will. One of the main reasons I didn't press charges at the time was because I felt the church would provide justice instead of the 'world'; now it could look to people as though he's done nothing wrong, certainly nothing worthy of a custodial sentence. I would now say to Christian women out there if you love him, report him - keep records, take photos, carry a dictaphone, visit your doctor. Even if you have NO intention of leaving, then still keep records, dates, take photos, get things in doctors' records. I believe now that Christian ministers who find this out should advise (not force, as women who have been controlled need empowering) women to go to the police. My minister did this when I first spoke to him. His initial reactions were totally perfect. The only problem has always been the public issue of Rob's crimes and my safety. In retrospect the church admits the one thing over which it cannot truly empathise is the extreme fear faced by victims. At least I know that all mistakes have been made in ignorance and ignorance alone. Nobody needs tell me that going to the police is easier said than done, but in retrospect I so wish I had done this at the time instead of leaving it, maybe, just maybe for a later date. This has nothing to do with forgiveness. I have learned the big lesson that forgiveness and justice are not mutually incompatible.

I do feel this week I have entered a new stage of healing which is new and therefore a bit frightening to me, and that is passing and appropriate anger. The outreach service has been worried that all my anger is directed inwards at myself. To this day, I feel little anger with him, but I do find myself suddenly coming out with (for me) some quite outrageous comments, even to people in authority, and just completely not caring that I've done it. But the anger with Rob is only fleeting and it soon turned inwards and includes other 'unsavoury' things such as, on occasions, becoming preoccupied with self-harm. This is not, I should stress, in a suicidal way, but simply to 'cut out' the pain in a tangible way that I can feel and so that I'm in control of my body, whiles ironically abusing it as Rob did, so limited are my own skills in being able to express anger having had all emotions banned for so long.

I think in many practical ways I have moved on so fast in this first part of the journey, and want others to do the same. But I do have to learn to go slower, to be patient, let others catch up with me and learn that God is in control.

It is frustrating, but as a teacher I should know that people don't learn skills all in one go: they have to listen, maybe several times; they have to internalise; they have to think and pray, and only then can they act. And I shouldn't be impatient; I've learned to channel certain emotions one day only to appear to have 'lost' more skills the next. It's a bit like a game of snakes and ladders; I don't know where I'm going to climb or when I'm going to sink.

When people from church have prayed with me, they have always prayed that I will be able to show forgiveness. I can honestly say that I do not feel I would be alive today if I had not, every night, committed Rob to God, and asked for his forgiveness. Anger is something which I have felt very rarely in my life but suddenly, quite out of the blue this week, I thought: Rob, this is all your fault, you have ruined my life, not me, you. This is progress, apparently. But it's only ever happened this once, so far, and it disappeared as quickly as it appeared. But with this goes fear about the future and the questions asked over and over again: Will my friends really stick by me? Will I really continue to have the good social life I've always had? What about the church? Will it be too much? I know I'm like a stuck record, but so is my life; just going on and on, round and round, backwards and forwards, sometimes tolerable, sometimes almost too much.

Chapter Seventeen

The end of this week marks the start of ten days called 'on the wings of a dove' which is run by the World Council of Churches and is aimed at educating churches on domestic violence. In the booklet that accompanied the leaflets, there's a section on forgiveness. It's only just occurred to me that when you feel anger then alongside that must often be an element of unforgiveness. This booklet says: "Often the church has expected women to forgive all too easily and go back to a violent or abusive relationship with no reason to believe that there is repentance or a change of heart on the part of the abuser or violent partner."

I believe there are 'levels' of forgiveness. When I forgave Rob, I knew he would hurt me all over again. People, even in the church, make assumptions about forgiveness, something which no one should *ever* do, unless that person has opened up to you about where they are in the process, and should also never 'preach' it at you if they (most likely) have absolutely no idea what you have been through and cannot even begin to empathise.

A woman who pioneers work in America on domestic violence and Christianity argues that forgiveness is the last step; she maintains that there are certain preconditions to forgiveness and the most important of these is justice. Drawing on such scriptural passages as Micah 6 v 8 (the call to do justice, love mercy and walk humbly with God) the church must make justice central. This means that abusers must be prepared to show genuine repentance and make retribution. Forgiveness by an abused partner may only come later. People who are recovering from abuse are often burdened by unreasonable expectations on the part of other people who want them to give and forget, but forgiveness comes at the final stage of a long process through which victims gain control of their own lives. Moreover, she argues, forgiveness only becomes an option if some form of justice is done. I do not necessarily agree with this as Rob has faced no justice whatsoever, continues to be in complete denial and completely unrepentant - I only need to receive solicitors' letters to see that - yet I have still forgiven him at the only level my heart, soul and mind can comprehend right now, in the confusion of incredible trauma, stress and mixed emotions which torment me with love and an imaginary, perfect marriage.

I have heard from people that he is a 'broken man.' Fortunately, I do not have to worry about whether this is true. He has lost my professional salary, a house, and a social group. I'm quite sure that when I'm sitting here loving him after all I've been through, he has little, if any, love or sense of loss from a relationship that never really was - because I'm the one manufacturing that, not him. But I do know if he were a truly, broken man, a broken man ready to be mended, I would be the first to know, because with real brokenness comes real conviction and real sorrow, and I would be the one who would be on the receiving end. Instead, I continue to be on the receiving end of fraud, and psychological and financial abuse through the legal channels. So Rob is still at it - this time charming his way into the hearts of people who witnessed his behaviour, and always previously saw straight through him, whilst I sit alone in the only place I know is safe, deep in the recesses of my numbed mind.

To forgive someone is not to let them off the hook - it's to transfer them to God's hands as the righteous judge of all human beings. Forgiving doesn't mean pretending that you're not hurt. On the cross, Jesus said 'Father, forgive them, for they don't know what they are doing'(Luke 23 v 34 Holy Bible). And yes, Rob did know what he was doing, but if hurt is ongoing, then forgiveness needs to be too; every time I write a card that just has my name on, every time I come to an anniversary, every time I buy a ready meal, just for one, every time I know 'our' group is meeting and I'm here alone because Rob has uncomfortably infiltrated my friendship group, albeit temporarily … Hurt needs to be eventually left behind in order to move on. We can't build a new life whilst we are still tied by unforgiveness to the old. However, what people need also realise is that an inability to move on does not mean that forgiveness has not taken place – that is far too simplistic. Jesus was still nailed to the cross and tortured after he forgave those who were abusing him.

Some wise people at church have always said that really I should have gone to the police and pressed charges, because when I was saying I loved Rob, but I had done nothing about it, this was inconsistent. After all, this is one of the difficulties I say I have with the church and yet I am doing the same thing. Another friend spoke to me a couple of weeks ago about sharing my difficulties with the home group (this is a small, close-knit group within the church – I belonged to a different one back then). I felt I could not do this without getting too emotional, and felt it was too big a burden to place on her, so I asked an acquaintance to do it instead. Obviously I wasn't there, but I had a phone call the next day saying how upset she was he had gone into details. I hadn't been into any details with this person, who is more of an acquaintance, and finally established that what she meant was that he mentioned we had separated through domestic violence.

This is one of my greatest difficulties.

How many times have we been helped, encouraged, or strengthened through hearing what God has done in the lives of other people, usually through difficult circumstances? But no one wants to know. I *still* feel as though I have a dirty secret that no one else must ever find out about, and to a certain extent, this prevents my healing.

And yet at the same time, without my faith, my family, my Christian friends and my church, I would have absolutely nothing now to live for. At this morning's service there was a lovely reading, entitled 'Faith is' (again from the book by Pamela Reeve). Four things in particular struck me:

Firstly, 'Faith is remembering I am indispensable to God when I feel I just clutter up the landscape.' Secondly, 'Faith is remembering I am God's priceless treasure when I feel utterly worthless.' Thirdly, 'Faith is confidence in God's faithfulness in an uncertain world on an uncharted course through an unknown future', and finally, 'Faith is leaving those we love to God to sort out.' I believe that eventually other people are going to find healing in my wounds. My greatest life messages and my most effective ministry will come out of my deepest hurts. There are plenty of people who are all too quick to point out weaknesses, they may, or may not be true, but I am learning to fill my heart with praise for Jesus who understands my every weakness.

Is it me that is not ready? Or is it the church that's not ready to hear? However much love I feel, do we still belong to the 'it doesn't happen here' brigade? Maybe it's because people know Robert. But where would many of us be today if we hadn't heard the testimonies of people who suffered at the hands of others? In fact, no one would be saved if they weren't prepared to think about the violence and abuse that Jesus went through on our behalf. I don't know why I was called to go through so much when I already have so much to contend with physically, but I do know that the verse from 2 Corinthians 12 v 9, Holy Bible is the same today as it was all those years ago: "My grace is sufficient for you, for my power is made perfect through weakness."

In the words of a lady who was telling her story recently about how she was raped in her own bedroom by a stranger, I now too belong to a secret club that I wish I didn't belong to and the pain of being in that club will never ever go away. But if I'd never been there, I would never have been able to fulfil the plans I know God has for my life.

I close my chapter with this: when I got home from church, knowing that they were not ready to hear what I feel increasingly is my dirty secret, I had an e-mail from Christian policewoman whom I had e-mailed several weeks previously. She asked so innocently, 'Vicky, your e-mail really moved me. Please can I use it in my presentations to try and educate churches on the reality of what goes on out there?'

'Yes please,' I replied, and not only that, I was then asked for my testimony to go in a national Christian newspaper. Other parts of my story are now being used around churches in not just England, but also abroad in Kenya, Geneva and elsewhere (and also in a domestic violence and disability study) to help educate, and help alert the church to the reality of what goes on, not just 'out there' but 'in here' too.

I am thankful to God that there are people out there who are determined that churches will be educated, and I have determined too, to be part of that process, so that my greatest life's message and my most effective ministry will come out of my deepest hurts.

Chapter Eighteen

Just as everyone was saying 'you're looking better', wham, it hit me! People don't realise that reactions are reactions of fright and terror - people have challenged me on, though not accused me of, all sorts of things that are fear driven, such as not coping with going out, or going to church, or work, because they cannot understand the intense fear that accompanies domestic violence. Sometimes my brain and mind felt as though they were going into emotional overload. The problem with each major attack of depression is, because it is part of post-traumatic stress rather than a clinical illness, I've not been able to see it coming. And if you're already dead on the inside, what's the point in being alive, robotic, a shell on the outside?

I knew that God wouldn't want my life to end, as I firmly believe that my times are in his hands - He decided when I would be born and will decide when I will die. But it was when I was alone, at those deepest times, separated from friends and a social life that was once busy and constant, that I started to doubt. I'm a people person - I really need people around me. I don't do 'alone'. At times I felt let down by individuals or bodies of people, although in retrospect I recognise what a huge responsibility it is for untrained friends to spend time with someone who was as low as I was (except that if someone had actually explained that at the time to me, and given me other suggestions or contacted professionals on my behalf, instead of just appearing to ignore me, then my whole life would have been better during those times). Communication is the key to everything. Rob ignored me. I had to beg him to help me many times when I was lying, helpless in my own vomit, on the floor. People, in general, just don't realise that it feels, at times, to a sensitive and terrorised person, that they are doing the same. I may understand now, but it mustn't be allowed to happen to others in the future.

There needs to be forgiveness – it's been harder than forgiving Rob. I learned to have low expectations of him so as not to be further disappointed; I thought more of the rest of my friends in all settings. I must acknowledge, though, that so many more people have been truly wonderful – it's so sad that the few negatives stick in your mind. It's not called unforgiveness – it's called depression – never get the two mixed up.

I know now they didn't understand. People were scared of pushing me over the edge – again. Although in reality it was not intentional, at the time I felt like the psalmist in Psalm 55 when he says: "If an enemy were insulting me I could endure it, but it is you, a man like myself, with whom I once used to enjoy fellowship as we walked to the house of God …", and also in Psalm 31 where he says: "I am an object of reproach, a laughing stock to my neighbours (actually my neighbours were great!), a dread to my friends; they who see me abroad flee from me, I am forgotten like the unremembered dead, I am like a dish that is broken." In my current negativity, I must acknowledge my actual neighbours – it's been like a 'soap' round here: people asking you in for lunch or popping in for a coffee, others noticing when your lights go on as a way of checking you're okay and driving home to find a neatly cut lawn. Small acts of kindness that make such a difference.

We all face losses daily to some extent, but so did Jesus. He accepts that my feelings are valid, simply on the basis that I feel them, which means they are not 'pathetic' or 'stupid' as Rob so often said.

Once Jesus had said his goodbyes, he had to walk the lonely road of abandonment. He knew he needed strength to endure the deep emptiness that awaited him – the emptiness of betrayal and loneliness. My keyworker once mentioned that she had rarely seen such a deep sadness in a person's eyes – this I believe was the sadness of loneliness in suffering, as much as it was abuse. Jesus asked his closest friends to stand by him as he struggled with his pain. How much more intense must Jesus' pain have been made by the fact that his friends didn't stand by him, didn't watch with him, as he agonised over his future. He loved them so much – yet they were not there just when he needed a friend to be there. Any time we face our own agony and we have to go it alone without loved ones to wait with us (and incidentally I must say that my family were totally and completely fantastic – better role models could never be found – but in practical terms they live some distance away) we stand in the place that Jesus stood when he agonised before his death, in the garden where he feared the inner void and pain that would be his.

Long before Jesus reached Calvary he was bruised, beaten, and battered by physical pain both from inside and outside. Like I felt. He had been betrayed by his friends. Like I felt, rightly or wrongly. He had been denied by others. Like me. Or like I felt. He had been treated like an inhuman object. Like me. He had seen the desolate compassion on his mother's face as she had to stand by, helpless. Like me.

Jesus was empty. His mother and brothers stood at the foot of the cross (praise God for families like mine) – but most of his friends were 'standing at a distance'.

He cried out his pain of desolation – this is like the cry of any of us who have faced a devastating separation in our lives, when overwhelming and overpowering feelings of loneliness, emptiness and abandonment rule everything. Where are you God when I need you so much? Why can't I feel your presence?

However, we are not left with Jesus' emptiness and desertion – if we were then there would be no point to anything.

Calvary is the deepest separation that anyone has ever known, far deeper than anything I went through, or may go through, whatever it feels like at the time, but the resurrection is the greatest new life or start that anyone could ever experience. As well as being the hope for all mankind, the resurrection is a special reminder that we too can be raised from the emptiness of loss.

Chapter Nineteen

December 2001

'This is the chapter you don't show anyone until you've moved past this point.' (Or in my case, until you think you have – I went lower after this after several good months.) It's about nine weeks since the injunction. I've moved through elation, worry as to whether I have done the right thing, loneliness, emptiness, shame, and, at times, a deep sense of peace in knowing that I have done the right thing.

My outreach worker has been concerned that when I relate painful experiences, my voice goes wobbly, my eyes fill with tears, and then I immediately pull back, relating the most awful scenarios whilst giggling. She feels it's very important to let go, and cry. I am frightened that if I let go my feelings will get out of control, or that I might explode or go crazy. For such a long time I have been avoiding thinking about traumatic events; at times I have become numb to stop myself from feeling anything, to let myself float away like I did during the worst assaults. In our sessions together over the last few weeks I have managed what I have called 'controlled crying'. Maybe it's called that anyway, but I feel that because I have not been allowed to express my emotions without being mocked or laughed at, or told how extra unattractive and unlovable I look, crying feels like a new experience to me, and one that, for the time being, makes me feel that I am sinking lower into depression than it does a release. It is an enormous compliment to her and her endless patience that I now feel safe to cry just a little in our sessions, and since then I have been able to recognise, at least from time to time, that this is not my fault, and under no circumstances do I deserve the treatment and the abuse that I received.

However, I now feel I have reached the next stage of post-traumatic stress: the big D – depression.

I was depressed when I was still with Rob, but because I had to be alert and on guard all the time, I had a little bit of reserve left to keep me fighting – it simply was not safe to sink right down. Although I'm still frightened, I know that there are systems in place which are for my protection. I know that post-traumatic stress is a completely normal reaction to crimes of violence and abuse and that all who suffer physical injury or threat to life will develop signs of this, in the short term at least. And the thoughts of self-injury (not of death) are all-consuming at times – mainly those times in the evenings when I'm expecting to go out socially, and realise I am all alone. Some of the paperwork I have been given says that some of these signs may go after a week or two, but others may stay for months or years, especially if the violence and threats have been repeated.

Although I am generally still constantly anxious, I have had only one of what I call genuine panic attacks, where my pulse races and I think I'm going to die, in the whole twelve weeks. This is amazing considering that I had a minimum of one panic attack a day, and woke up with one virtually every night for at least the last two years.

However, the depression that is haunting me now, and has been getting worse for the last three weeks, is like nothing I've ever experienced before, despite having thought that I knew what it was like. Before, when I was still married and felt desperate, I wanted to be with people, I wanted to be distracted, and this always, at least in part, lifted the worst of it.

Three weeks ago I was worried about losing my friends, about losing my church; now I just want to be on my own. I have sat on the sofa several times not noticing that six or seven hours have passed, that it has got dark, that there are messages on the phone, that I haven't eaten anything all day. Even my family, who are my best friends not just my relatives, have offered to come over and stay, but I have turned them down. I feel that I have lost interest in everything, and even the prospect of recovering in order to become an adoptive parent feels irrelevant and uninteresting. The only thing I've wanted in thirty-four years of life is to be a mum. Even though this is a realistic dream, it just seems too far away, and I feel that the likelihood of me surviving intact for that long is just ridiculous and totally unachievable.

I have to admit that I have found my mind wandering towards that storage box full of medication. I wouldn't do anything, anyway I'm so tolerant of my medication, but at least I know my body will tolerate taking high doses that will make me sleep all weekend so that time goes by more quickly. I never know whether if I hibernate I'll wake up one day and feel better or whether I have to go through this head-on in order to come out the other side. I guess really I know the answer, but it is too much to face right now.

I'm very clumsy in the kitchen and am always having accidents because of my spasms. I must admit that having cut my finger just slightly on a serrated knife, and seeing how much blood came out from something that hardly hurt at all, it did occur to me just how easy it would be to slip slowly away through blood loss and probably without any pain. I could always wrap myself up tightly in bandages and put on a nice jumper so I wouldn't look horrible to whoever found me, so that my family's last memories would be spared from the sight of blood and gore. It frightened me then, as it does still now, that I actually seriously contemplated how I could do away with myself. Or there's always blocking up the exhaust pipe of my car – I've heard that's not unpleasant.

As a Christian, I know full well it is up to God when I was born and when I will die, but knowing how wonderful heaven must be doesn't really help when I'm stuck down here, where I don't want to be. I can still just about think outside of my own little bubble to realise how painful it would be (for some unearthly reason) for my family to cope with that situation, especially when to a certain extent I have chosen to push them out for their protection.

Before Rob went travelling round the world, a couple of weeks after the injunction, I heard that he had got another job down here. This job is about fifteen miles away as far as I know, but he has chosen to rent a room at a mutual friend's, which is the closest he could possibly be to me, being less than two minutes' drive away. What makes this more ironic is the fact that there are plenty of other options open to him, and when he stayed at this friend's before he had nothing good to say about his living conditions, yet he has chosen those and I can't help feeling that this is to intimidate and abuse me from 'afar'– just cleverly enough so that he is not breaking the terms of the injunction.

Last weekend, when I knew he was coming back from his travels, I got so anxious on top of the depression that I couldn't stop shaking. For the first time ever, I had to phone a doctor on Sunday who advised me that I could take a much higher dosage of my morphine based painkiller than it says on the leaflet. However, the next morning I was still in agony so I went to Casualty and spent most of the day drugged up to the eyeballs in the ward next door.

To add insult to injury, my original outreach worker announced that week that she has been promoted to her manager's position whilst she is away on maternity leave. I'm really pleased for her – I have spoken to all the other keyworkers on the phone at various times, and they all sound very similar to each other in the way that they are very softly spoken, kind and gentle, but it still didn't surprise me to find that I obviously had the best worker. I could genuinely say that I know she deserves it, but it leaves me feeling incredibly unsupported at the very time when I need her most, simply because I am learning to cry and express anger in a place and with a person who makes me feel safe enough to slowly let out my feelings. And Rob is just about to come back. And the post-traumatic stress is kicking in. They are a fantastic organisation, and of course they would never leave you high and dry, and immediately find you someone else, but this reaction is just an example that goes to show how 'close to the edge' we live, when we finally escape. And how much we need other people in all capacities, from all walks of life.

It's just that sometimes I feel that it always happens to me and it's not fair. Please, Lord, help me not to get cynical.

A lovely reading today - God always sends me the right words for the right occasion. "Faith is ... confidence in God's faithfulness to me in an uncertain world, on an uncharted course, towards an unknown future - reliance on the certainty that God has a purpose for my life when everything seems meaningless, resting in the fact that God has an objective in leaving me on the scene when I feel useless to Him and a burden to others." ('Faith is')

During the latest three or four weeks, I have slowly climbed upwards again, on occasions to the point of normality, but then almost as quickly seem to wake up and be once again in a pit of despair. I had a lot of dreams and nightmares about Rob over the last few nights, mainly of him being a baby and me bringing him up, teaching him how to live and love.

I have found this weekend particularly hard although I have not been short of things to do. One good thing is that I can cry, I can cry alone, and although I have cried on and off much of the weekend, I can stop, I'm not going mad or crazy and I'm not going out of control. Also, I feel a deep sense of sadness rather than hopelessness, which means that no silly thoughts of self-harm etc. are going through my mind. Maybe it's turning into a more normal sort of grief?

I went to church this morning, the first time for probably four weeks. I did this because my class were doing a nativity play in the service and they needed an extra pair of hands to help them get changed. It doesn't seem to matter what I do on Sundays, I always feel terrible. On Sundays, I always love Rob, I always want to go and see him, I always want to text him, I always think about cuddling him, and lying there next to him in bed, or snuggled up tight and warm. It's almost too much to speak these words without getting in my car and going to find him before it's too late. I don't know how I will ever be able to put pen to paper to sign any divorce papers. I thought these feelings had gone, and they are just feelings, and they are just in my imagination, because the only time I've snuggled up in bed with Rob was long before we moved and he came down to stay in my flat at weekends. So again this is the marriage of my imagination, but imagination (or rather, desperately wanting to see the beauty and goodness in someone, and forgetting the bad side, the side that ruled ninety-nine per cent of our marriage) can be very strong, and very real.

It's so weird, but one minute I can be avoiding anything and everything to do with Rob and our marriage, to the point of numbness where all thoughts are persistently blocked out, and, just when I think I have 'frozen', some bizarre thought pops into my head, like the other day when I suddenly, and apparently out of the blue thought 'I do hope Robert's eating enough vegetables!' Then I go over and over things in my head and relive events over and over and over again. I still don't want to go out, although I can manage specific places, like people's homes – it's wide, open, unpredictable places I can't cope with. I still haven't made an effort to do anything much social, and the fact that I don't care worries me, although when friends have called on me, or dragged me out, I feel loads better afterwards.

What makes this weekend particularly difficult is that on Tuesday, in two days time, it is Rob's birthday. He's always been very childlike about his birthday, getting excited for months beforehand and expecting huge presents and special treats. What I find especially difficult is that he will be living down here, two minutes away, with mutual friends who can all send him cards and celebrate, and here's me, his wife, unable to do anything in case it is misinterpreted or adds to his confusion. If he couldn't understand love when I gave two hundred per cent, there is no possibility of understanding it now.

I just spoke to Mum, who as usual had her pearls of wisdom. I was saying how weird it is that on Sundays I always love him so much. I guess on a Sunday, although my faith is something that I live, or try to live throughout the week, on a Sunday I see Rob more as God sees him, with all the potential, and the flashbacks of those few times when I could see what he could be if he chose to let go of his abusive ways. I was saying to Mum how I have long accepted that this is the end of the relationship, but today my sadness is a different sort of sadness, more like grief and bereavement. In relation to sending him a card, she so wisely said that, if something is going to happen then it has to be unprompted, it has to be a complete turnaround, and I firmly believe that if I'm not supposed to sign those divorce papers, then God will act in a miraculous way in His time, not in mine, not in Rob's, but in His.

When I spoke to the national twenty-four hour helpline earlier, they asked me what birthdays and special occasions had been like. This made me remember (I hadn't really forgotten - I think I was just choosing to) that in actual fact birthdays had been really awful times for me. I've just been looking through the records that I kept over the past years, and they hardly paint a glowing picture of happy birthdays.

> "Sunday the 8th of July 1999 was a bad time. Shane had rung at lunchtime to ask if we were doing anything later. I said that no, we were both free, although I was going to church, but that was all. We arranged that they would come round about 7.30 p.m. Robert was furious that I had said that I was going to church and started shouting and saying that he hadn't seen Shane for ages and it was rude of me. I said that I had every intention of seeing him and that I'd be back for when

they got in – and that I would leave church early. I had all the 'I expect you as my wife to be here'. This went on and on. Fortunately, we had promised them pizza, so I decided to go against all my principles and use that as an excuse to creep in to the first part of the church service as well. He had also been having a go at me earlier in the weekend for having told him I'd arranged a surprise for his birthday which just included the two of us. He said I was selfish and should think of it from his point of view! I had tried to e-mail the hotel to see if I could cancel, so that he could decide whether he wanted to go or not. However I hadn't told him this, because I was too scared and waiting for the proverbially right moment.

Once out of the house I was trembling and tearful, and knew that if I went to church then I would tell everyone as the love there would make me spill the beans, so I just sat outside in the car. I suddenly felt an absolute terror about going home, so I dropped a note through Elsie's door – it went something like 'please pray for me, Rob got furious when I said I wanted to go to church tonight as Shane and Eva are coming round, and his temper is like nothing you could imagine. I feel really scared to go home, please would you pray for me.' I think I felt sufficiently scared to ask her to phone me on my mobile the next day to ensure that I was okay.

I drove home, and sat outside in the car till I saw Shane draw up, so that we should go in together.

Shane happened to mention Rob's birthday and he said that he thought I had something organised and that it was a bit controversial. I said that I had e-mail to the man to see if we could cancel what we were doing as Rob hadn't been keen. He immediately said that wasn't the sort of thing I should tell him in public and that we would talk about it later. That made my stomach sink like it's never sunk before. I knew that the abuse would start the second they had gone - how selfish I've been, how inconsiderate to have arranged a surprise, how I shouldn't have brought it up in front of them (well, they did actually) and he was ranting and raving (and if I'd heard this going on next door it was bad enough that I'd have called the police). He even started throwing china pasta bowls onto the floor, aiming for my feet and legs, where they smashed. He then changed the subject rapidly, as he does, and out of nowhere started saying how it was all to do with the cats and how he hated them and how he wanted them out of the house in twenty-four hours or else he would take them to the sanctuary or throw them out to fend for themselves because they were the root cause of everything, and that I was never allowed to mention them again, or look at any photos of them, which I would have to get rid of. You know, he then started shouting at me and swearing again and told me what a selfish b**** I was for arranging his birthday surprise, and what a nightmare I am to live with, and how I need to make more of an effort because things I do like that are making him angry. This lasted for over two hours, and I had another collapsing/sick turn, which he said I did for effect and I was filthy and disgusting. I pleaded with him that at that point I needed to sleep, it was past 11 p.m. I am not allowed to talk to him at all to raise big issues in the evening because he is so tired. If I say that I'm tired and must go to sleep (sometimes my walking deteriorates to crawling point through tiredness and stress) yet he will just ignore it, even if I beg to be allowed to go to bed. Anyway, eventually I was left with an ultimatum to not come home the next day until I came back to collect the cats to take them away.

Anyway, that night when he was asleep I went down and took my spare car keys off his keyring. This was not to be vindictive, but because I felt my only refuge where he couldn't hurt me was my car, and I didn't want him to have access to it. I also knew he wouldn't notice it had gone – which he didn't for weeks.

In the morning, I packed a bag with everything important and locked it in the boot of my car, just in case I needed to run fast. I also made a list of things I'd like to additionally take if there was time. I don't mean 'leaving' as in divorce, but just in case I felt unsafe to stay temporarily.

I visited Elsie the next day and we talked and prayed through everything – although I could not possibly tell her how bad things were – I worry they would give a heart attack! I was so relieved when she said that I'm not responsible for Rob's temper, and that it's not me who is affecting his spiritual development, which is another thing he constantly says. Also, whenever I asked to read or pray together, he says he'll see if my behaviour improves over the next fortnight and then he'll 'reassess'. I have always been told the same by friends, counsellors, church leaders, but it's though there's a mental block, 'wanting' Rob to be right and me to be wrong.

Elsie suggested I spoke to the ministers of the church, but I said I'd feel like a traitor. I suddenly realised how late it was and how Rob would have been home hours, so I went outside and phoned him and asked him if I would be safe if I went home. Four times he put the phone down on me, and on the fifth attempt he picked it up and said that of course I was safe; the cats were fine and not be so silly, although he did still expect me to 'sort' the cats. (Bad luck Rob – today they're happily running round 'our'/my house – that was the one and only 'rule' I had no problems immediately breaking!) Anyway, having cancelled my surprise birthday weekend for Rob he said that his best treat would be for me to 'b***** off' and that he'd rather spend his birthday without me. But I knew he'd want some sort of treat, even if he didn't want me, and after all, he hadn't asked for a surprise, had he? Today I wish I'd gone away for the weekend and not arranged anything – but that's retrospective. Much too dangerous at the time. Rereading now, I can see how simple it must sound to other people if you've not been there.

So, at short notice I ran down a list of pubs I know he likes and got together a group of us to go out on Saturday night. Several people came round in the afternoon, and Robin, in front of Rob, asked if we could call round for him so that he could follow us in his car. We were picking Shane and Eva up, and he was planning to follow behind with the others. As we drove down the road, instead of turning right to Shane's house, I first went left to Robin's, as this was the agreed plan. Rob, like a flick of a switch, screamed so loudly that I had palpitations and nearly drove into a wall, as he said, 'Pick up Shane – what are you doing?' I replied that I was going to Robin's as arranged and he was screaming 'Stupid b**** – do what you're told!'

Fortunately he had to shut up as the two roads are only metres apart, and fortunately everyone that truly confirmed that I'd done it right without knowing how helpful that was! I was shaking like a leaf and crying when we picked them up, but fortunately it was dark. When we got to the pub in the middle of a country lane, Rob just sat on the comfy seat while I sat alone on an uncomfortable stool still shaking, and I was really tempted just to leave, go home, grab extra bits and pieces and flee. I had even booked the cats into the cattery earlier in the week just in case I had to leave and couldn't take them. I have never felt so close to doing that as it would have been ages before he noticed I had gone, but I didn't want to shame him in front of all our friends. He wondered later on why ever I had been so quiet. Such is my lot."

Every year I've done something wrong on his birthday. Last year during an air show he commented how much he would enjoy a helicopter ride. I tried like mad to book a helicopter flight for his birthday, but just couldn't. Eventually I found a friend of a friend who would take him up in his small plane and help him to fly himself, and fly back over our house and the surrounding areas where he could video and take photos. Rob guessed that I had some sort of airborne surprise for him this year, but when he opened the envelope and saw that it was an aircraft instead of a helicopter, he was quite open in expressing his disappointment towards me and then demanded I gave him the money I would have spent in order to buy him a fourth drill! (At least I made sure I kept that for myself when the time came for him to move his things out!)

So, here I am being miserable about birthdays, but in retrospect, he's got exactly what he wants. Nearly every year he has said something to the effect of his best birthday treat being that I'd 'b***** off' somewhere, so now I hope his wish has come true. It's true, writing is therapeutic, and it also brings reality home, however painful reality is, but I know one thing, I think I'll just leave that birthday card!

So yes, Jesus in Gethsemane was a man at the end of his emotional resources, with friends too scared to say anything lest they 'rocked the boat'. He had faced up to the emotional reality that betrayal was coming – not from one of his worst enemies, but from one of his closest friends. It would be blasphemous to say that I understand what Jesus went through – all I know is that I've been pushed beyond my emotional limits to a point at which I felt the pain would kill me. I've felt that only physical death could release me from the pain of emotional agony. If Jesus faced this, then of course, we can too. But God gave Jesus the strength to continue. I was at the end of my emotional resources too. But God knows and understands every darkest experience we go through. That's why I believe that only He can help. He knows what it's like.

Chapter Twenty

Well, it's quite amazing, but having survived one anniversary, I feel the strongest I felt, not just since the injunction, but since I had counselling with Gill and realised that there was nothing I could do to change my situation.

I think it helped me to get through Rob's birthday as I went to see a friend's new baby the very same day - something both beautiful to me, and something bringing back painful and poignant memories of trying to get pregnant, for many months, with no (for which, in retrospect, I thank God) success. It may be my lifelong desire, but with it I'd never be allowed any closure and supposing I'd then had the courage to leave? Or had children also caught in the trap? Or had a little boy who turned into either a timid, scared teenager or a public 'charmer' who went home to beat up his girlfriend? It is true that in our Christian journey we walk by faith and can't always see the next step. We don't understand the 'why' questions but can see God revealing, bit by bit, the reasons why. I say we had no success, but I did once go for some forty plus days, and experienced morning sickness, but soon after discussing this with Rob, I did something 'wrong', I can't even remember what, possibly nothing at all, but got elbowed extremely hard in the low stomach (which wasn't a usual point of impact) and the next day I remember bleeding very heavily and very suddenly. I remember phoning the duty doctor who said that if it was a miscarriage there was nothing I could do. What I didn't tell her, of course, was the truth. Such a major part of my life, but something I could never share - the most precious thing - the thing I've always lived for - there one minute, gone the next, 'removed' by a father God knew it was better never became one, lost from a mother who could never have wanted anything more. So important, yet so insignificant; a potential life, removed in one small paragraph. I go back to my mention of Job in the Bible and to that New Year's prayer that I found, and how Job said, and I prayed I could too, after losing everything he had: "The Lord gave, and the Lord has taken away. May the name of the Lord be praised."

In the next week I had some particularly bad medical problems, including a probable prolapsed disk from where I had had very uncontrolled spasms the weekend Rob moved back down to Devon, but in myself I felt great. In terms of my self-esteem and my self-worth, confidence and guilt, I have huge strides I need to make, and the smallest things knock me back, but in myself I feel happy and content. I don't feel that deep depression; I certainly don't feel that deep hopelessness of only a few weeks ago. I even plucked up the courage to meet with my new key worker. Admittedly it was more difficult than I had expected once I arrived, but I did it, and I'll continue to do it, and pray that it gets easier week by week.

I wondered whether my coping strategies would continue over Christmas 2001 or whether this would be a time when I would again sink to my lowest. However, I am writing this after Mum has been staying for four days, and today we have had a houseful, and then suddenly they have all gone and I am on my own.

When you live in a situation such as mine, you forget the little things, the things that have actually made us laugh rather than cry. This year Rob and I were supposed to be having his whole family here over Christmas, something so bad it is what horror movies are made of!

One of the best things of all is that when I saw my lovely family all pile into my brother-in-law's car a couple of hours ago, although I felt sad to see them go, I knew I could shut the front door and that I would not have to face the fear of all that I had done wrong over the preceding days – not knowing whether the things were bad enough for a lecture, a two hour screaming fit where china was thrown around, a pint of water in the face, a kick in the ribs, or an 'accidental' push on the stairs, or when I was chopping with a sharp knife. Even more was the fear that for a few hours, maybe even a few days, everything would seem okay; I would just get the silent treatment, with my stomach doing a 'roller coaster' almost wanting to precipitate the inevitable, just to get it over with.

I didn't get hundreds of pounds worth of presents this year, although I got some lovely things, but I did get quality time and I got loads of love. I had my home open Christmas Day for those who had nowhere else to go, and this is the nicest Christmas I have had since meeting Robert.

Both Mum and my sister said at separate times how they realised in retrospect how tense they had been previous years when opening presents and when watching others opening theirs. I guess everyone develops their own family tradition. One of ours has always been to put some cryptic clue on the label as to what the present inside will contain. Even when I knew what was inside my presents because I had asked for them, we all had to be very careful not to make comments such as, 'oh yes, I remember now, I know what this is,' or something similar, because Rob would get very angry. Not only would he be annoyed with me, but sometimes he would 'have a little word with me' in the kitchen, telling me to speak to my relatives about their behaviour or they would not be welcome again. This would happen even if we were in my mother's house, or if it were nothing to do with me or my presents.

This year, because we had people we didn't know well for lunch and we had to drop them home, it was nearly six o'clock before we sat down to open our presents. I would not have been allowed to do this with Rob; in effect he was like a toddler when it came to presents. I remember he always wanted expensive presents, and I always felt obliged somehow to buy them because if might win his approval and he might be pleased with me – just for a few hours – maybe. Last year he wanted a memory stick for his laptop, and also an external floppy disk drive. Between them these came to over £150. Seeing as Rob always complains about my underwear (or any of my clothes) I asked him if he could buy stuff that he liked. He had never done this before – after a relationship of over five years he had to ask me for my size, but at least he did it. We opened our presents before we drove up to his family up north. When his parents rang, not particularly to wish us a happy Christmas but to see what we'd got, Rob complained that he only had two presents from me, whereas he'd given me about seven. This was obviously because each item was smaller, but it was as if he really couldn't see this; that he really thought that a bra and a memory stick were of equal value! (They probably are nowadays – but they actually weren't back then!) Of course I didn't mind, I was thrilled to get something personal, even though I had been very specific and told him exactly what I wanted, I just couldn't believe his attitude, especially when I had got him a good-quality item instead of the much cheaper version that I could have got.

Robert also used to get furious about me wanting to go to the watch night service on New Year's Eve. We would inevitably be at a party and people would be saying, 'shall we go?' or 'shan't we go?' I began to dread people asking me because I knew Rob didn't want to go but thought he would prefer this to going home where his friends weren't. Every year when people asked me what I wanted to do, I tried a different tactic, usually the one that Rob had asked me to use the year before. I tried diverting the question to him, then he would just glare at me because I should know the answer. If all our friends would say that they were going, then I would say I was going too, partly because I wanted to, and partly because I knew Rob would want to be with our friends, but it was always wrong.

One April I remember him in the middle of a two hour screaming session about how I was a nightmare, how my behaviour was terrible, how I couldn't compromise, how I always did things to upset him. On this occasion he was in the bath and I wasn't so I felt able to 'push' him. His standard response to, 'Please can you give me an example?' was a very loud, 'I don't have to justify myself,' to which, on this occasion, I said, 'Yes you do, because if I know what's upset you I can try not to do it again.' After a two hour discussion, which for some reason had started when Mum texted me to ask what time we would be picking her up the following morning for my niece's dedication (he would always leave arrangements to the last minute, because he knew it would stress me and other people involved), he said, 'Okay then, I will give you an example, an example of outrageous behaviour where you never take my feelings into account.' This 'outrageous behaviour' then turned out to be the fact that I had joined in a discussion about attending the watch night service at church, four months previously, before returning to our party and had gone to it with our friends (bearing in mind that I had only been brave enough to agree because that's what everyone else was doing, and therefore I thought Rob would want it too). I think this is one of the times when I realised that however near I got to his idea of perfection then the goalposts would move, in order that I should always fail. I now understand that this is all 'classic abuser behaviour'.

And yet … I'm still left with the guilt. But this week I have not only moved along a few squares, I have certainly not moved back any, in fact I think of gone up a fairly medium-sized ladder, and I'm proud, proud when I think of how far I have come in such a short space of time.

I am aware that at the top of each ladder is that snake's head which could so easily and quickly take me down again. I am sure that I will have to travel down some of them, but some of them I will miss, some of them I will struggle past, some of them I will jump over. I still don't know, but what I do know is that right now I am much closer to survivor than I am victim, and what's more, for the first time in my whole life, I am proud to be where I am today.

And, although my faith is not just for happier times, the reality of it has been tested through the more difficult times. When, at age seven, I just wanted to know that God would help me be brave enough to open my mouth at the dentist; now, when I reach out my hand in faith or put it into the hands of Jesus, the hands that were scarred for me, and hold it just for the next day, next hour, next minute, I am safe. He can cope with the future that I don't yet need to know. Rob may have to explain his plans and actions to me, but God does not because His ways are perfect and He is always working for my best.

Chapter Twenty-One

I had the privilege this week of writing the prayer diary that goes on the back of the church notice sheet each week. This is the song I put for December 31st 2001:

"I do not know what lies ahead, the way I cannot see,
but One stands near to be my guide, He'll show the way to me.
I know who holds the future, and He'll guide me with His hand,
with God things don't just happen, everything by Him is planned.
So, as I face tomorrow, with its problems large and small
I'll trust the God of miracles, give to Him my all."

(Alfred B Smith and Eugene Clark 1958,
Admin in the UK by Unisong Music Publishers)

I have never really been one to question things. I have always had a certain strength in accepting whatever comes my way, as I believe God has a purpose in everything.

For example, every day my pain seems to get worse, my mobility seems to decrease, but I have never felt angry or even the need to question God as to 'why me?' Maybe I can understand my pupils that little bit better, maybe I can empathise with their parents, maybe I can be the person that people come to when they have a problem (and they did always used to).

But now, for the first time in nearly thirty-five years of my life I want to know why? Not why has a disaster happened to me, my faith in God can cope with that, not really even why did I get hurt, shouted at, abused? What I want to know is why, why, why do I still have to love him so much? Mostly I know it is the image I love, but I love the potential that Rob could have, if only, only he would drag himself out of the pit of self-denial. I alternately want to throw my arms round him, scream at him, hurt him, shake him, but only to make him listen, to make him be what God wants him to be, and I want to scream at God too, less for what I have lost, and more for what Rob has lost.

I went to my solicitor's today, and it seems as though everything is going to be okay, with the house and all that; I don't need to worry. I am so pleased that the financial settlement will be done soon, while the divorce will still take weeks if not months. I want that to take forever - just in case. Its funny how you can trick yourself into believing that something's going to happen whilst knowing at the same time it's absolutely a no go area.

Why did we have to have such lovely wedding anniversary? It wasn't as though God knew that one of us was going to die or something so that we needed to have lovely memories. Instead, on the 21st February 2001, after a somewhat strained evening out, Robert admitted, in a rare moment of passion - in fact, the last time we were ever intimate (although at least I will always remember that that last time was his initiative and his love, which was unlike most of our 'encounters') - he admitted that he was to blame for all our problems, and he admitted that he knew I was scared of him, but I had a right to be, and he knew it would take me a long time to trust him, but would I forgive him? I knew the words were the rehearsed words of a counsellor, but that didn't matter if the sentiments behind them were genuine.

I think that was the happiest moment of my life, as I actually lay there in his arms, crying and kissing forgiveness all over him.

Although only moments later he kicked me of out of bed and said that I needn't think that meant I could share 'his' bed, and if I even tried to get in it again, he would just get out and go somewhere else. And then, within days, it was all happening again, major screaming and humiliating sessions after minor misdemeanours, things I thought I could now admit to, like being too tired to pop into a friend's for a drink after a night out. I thought I would be allowed to express that then, after all he was my 'new' husband. It was only three or four weeks later that I took out the injunction, weeks after my precious husband had said the words I don't really know whether he really meant or tried to mean. I just wish I had never heard them, and thought that God was working a miracle, when He quite obviously wasn't. In all that I have been through, it feels like the cruellest thing that ever happened to me.

When I Left You

"the day I forgave you your abuse of me
that moment when I said 'I love you still'
the very second I saw through you
into peacefulness
that's when I left you and became free

it wasn't when you were hitting me
nor when you woke me in the night,
nor when you broke the kitchen table
or even when you infringed upon my rights

it was after.

when you cried and said you'd change
and I knew you couldn't even if you tried
I saw you and saw through you
into peacefulness

that's when I left you and became free."

Breaking Free from Partner Abuse, Morning Glory Press, 1993. Compiled by Mary Marecek

I went to see a new counsellor last week, one to whom I had spoken on the phone several weeks previously. When I arrived I said how different I was, how much progress I had made in such a short space of time. Within about ten minutes I was a crumpled heap, a complete wreck, realising how superficial the initial stages of healing can be - like a scab covering a wound that looks better, but soon as you go and scratch it, it bleeds everywhere, opens up again and is no better than it was in the first place.

I told her of my frustrations, particularly when older and wiser Christians tried to explain Rob's behaviour away in terms of illness or mental health problems; she explained it the best way anyone ever has, and really it's so simple: that although we change when we become Christians we still have our unique God-given personalities, and that includes our strengths and weaknesses. When we are under stress, because we are no more perfect than those who are not Christians (it's just that we have a saviour who takes all our weaknesses upon himself, should we be open about them), we all behave by showing our greatest weakness. And if that's physical violence, or abusive behaviour of any kind, then, as physical beings, those particular behaviours will always be shown first. So whilst this does not mean there is no hope for Robert, I believe realistically, and as a Christian, that at his greatest moments of stress he will always be tempted, at least, to react in an abusive manner, even if he is convicted by God that this is wrong.

And yes, I do still believe in a God of miracles, but unless I one day hear that there is a certain Robert Court standing at the front of churches and talking about his life as a wife abuser and how God has freed him and changed him, then I believe that this will always be a behaviour to which he resorts. I don't believe for one moment that God wanted me to stay in the relationship while it was so detrimental to me (and in many ways reinforcing for Rob, who I am sure thought he could get away with anything because of my disability and my beliefs in the sanctity of marriage).

I believe I have been incredibly fortunate that no one has urged or prayed, or promised reconciliation or even hopes of it, although we all believe that God can change people and pray this for him. I know that God is not telling me to go back to Rob. God wants me to leave the past behind, to let go and heal the memories and flashbacks that rekindle the terror, and walk into the future with God. I feel it is important that prayer for victims of domestic violence should focus on healing of body, mind and memories, plus forgiveness too, if this is an issue for you. But I also believe it should not focus on prayers for reconciliation, or things that could stop a woman's healing and place her again in the trap of potentially going back, something she may well have been wrestling with before realising that it is *never* God's will for a woman to return to a violent relationship. Yes, God can raise the dead, He can do the impossible, but even though we believe, most of us don't pray that God will raise our dead relatives! It's the same with domestic violence – by the time most women are able to act, they have, on average, experienced thirty-five serious assaults and are already a long way down the journey of accepting the partnership is over. Leaving is often the end result of a process that could have begun years, sometimes decades, ago. It's also the start of a new journey. So please don't sit there and pray for reconciliation. It's like sitting with a bereaved person and asking God to raise the dead. Hopefully some of you are starting to get the point?

Don't get me wrong. Some men can admit their failings, come out of denial and start a new life, and on occasions reconciliation may be possible. This is covered in the last section of this book.

I believe the divorce will go ahead, because Rob still is digging himself deeper and deeper into denial, but I just pray that one day I might hear about him, or read about him, and see that what I've been through, and what Sharon before me has been through, has not been in vain, because there is a man out there who is all the better for his own suffering, and I just pray that I'll still be around to see it.

I'm packing boxes, just one a day, it's all I can cope with, and, although he probably couldn't care less, each item is being packed with love, prayer, and usually wrapped in a kiss.

It's a question people are always asking – why does a God of love send suffering? I don't believe that God sends suffering, although I do believe that He allows it. We talked about abuse being a choice. We all have choices or we'd be robots and we all, at times, choose the wrong path. What parent has ever had to teach their child to be naughty? Even Jesus himself struggled with this before his crucifixion. As a Christian I know that when I suffer I have come face-to-face with a God who suffers pain and hurt with me, but also wants me to be free from it, a God who wants to be with me in my suffering, and I have been aware that He has been closer to me in this than my friends were before. Sometimes we have to lose everything we have before we feel God in His love reaching out to us, sticking closer to us than we can ever expect the best friends in the world to. I know that He will never let me down, I know that when He promises something He will stick by me whether I deserve it or not – He will not run away because He can't cope, or because I am depressed, or go round in circles; I could even shout and scream at Him and know that He still loves me. God is a refuge for the needy, a shelter from the storm, a shade from the heat, a friend who sticks closer than any brother. No matter how intense or searing the hurt of a loss is, we know that we do not need to be destroyed by it because God can help us recover hope, courage and direction in life and will be with us throughout whatever journey it is that we have to travel. For me, this hasn't meant that I have never had moments of feeling abandoned by God. I believe that these are human and natural responses to grief, but it does mean an ultimate hope, a hope and trust in Christ alone.

Chapter Twenty-Two

When I went for my very first lot of counselling, now nearly two years ago, I was initially desperate for someone to tell me that I was doing things wrong. That would have put me in control. I loved Rob so much that I would have gone to any lengths - nothing would have been too major for me to change in order that his behaviour also changed. But of course, in retrospect so obviously, each counsellor I went to (and I went to several in order to find one who would find that the blame lay with me) told me that there was absolutely nothing I could do.

I started having long absences from work, because the morning depression was so awful; I knew I would be okay at home, safe to have a relaxing bath, safe to go to sleep (I was sleeping between two and four hours a night at the time, and had been for two to three years), safe to be in my own home and enjoy it. Robert was working over 150 miles away each day at that time, and, seeing as he never asked about my day with any interest, he was unaware of just how little I attended work. In fact in one full academic year, I worked only four weeks full time. I never reached the lows I have reached since the injunction; I guess I needed to protect myself from sinking to the very bottom in case I needed to get away suddenly.

Robert found out about the counselling and was furious; he said it would take a very long time to forgive me for doing such an awful thing. He said that the marriage was between both of us, just two of us, and that we should sort it out alone. I was brave enough to say that we couldn't do this, it had gone too far. My original counsellor (to whom

I am forever grateful) insisted that I broke the confidence. She really felt strongly that I should go to the police, and in retrospect, I really wish I had. Instead, I chose someone who I thought Rob would really listen to because he would be ashamed of him knowing – and this was our minister at church. He was superb, very empathic, and incredibly understanding. His first instinctive reaction was that I should get out, at least temporarily, and that the church would stand by me whatever I did, being more concerned at a time like this for my physical and emotional safety than for Rob's spiritual wellbeing.

Once Robert found out that our minister knew, the physical attacks decreased immediately initially, although the emotional ones increased, with only three or four major assault incidents in the last year of our marriage. I was once brave enough to ask him how he had stopped being so physically 'inappropriate' as I called it, and he replied that he'd 'just decided'. Talk about choice! And he followed it up by saying that I hadn't shown enough gratitude – I hadn't thanked him for not hurting me! However, I don't know whether I noticed it more because things were less physical, or whether it had always been there at this intensity, but the psychological abuse then became intolerable. Our minister and his wife came round a few times, something I feel somewhat guilty about putting them through. The real issue was never tackled – I think they feared for my safety after they had left, so they directed the 'issues' at both of us, and we spent most of the time discussing how difficult it was for Rob living with a 'poor disabled wife' – one who worked sixty hours a week, cooked every meal, packed every lunch, washed every item of clothing – all on two hours' sleep a night, with constant abuse thrown in. I think when I say to people that the abuse was pretty much constant, they think this is an exaggeration; but as other abused women will tell you, we all tend to minimise what's happened to us, so badly do we want to see and remember only the good. For example, after our minister had spent a very long time explaining that compromise didn't mean both putting your point of view forward and then doing what you wanted, rather it meant meeting at a middle ground, and we then had to transfer this literally to every area of the house. I like to be cool at night (well I don't actually, but I always liked the window open in case I scream so that someone hears me) whilst Rob likes to be warm. So compromise, in his eyes, meant shutting the window! After this meeting we actually had to measure how wide the window opened in our bedroom, and have the halfway mark marked on the wall, so that we could make sure that we were compromising!

As life went on, I became more and more despondent that things would change. Many people prayed for a miraculous change in Rob's life. I waited. I prayed. I waited. Nothing happened. I came across more and more little but deceitful things that concerned me. Things like having store cards. Robert always wanted us to share cards, and it actually took me five years to realise that he had always taken the 'dominant' card, so that points I collected with my money went onto his card for him to spend. Only a small and trivial example, but the one thing Rob had always said was his strong point, was that he was very honest. I now realise, with great sadness and pity on his behalf, that these were the things that he craved, because deep down I guess he knew that his whole life was one big facade.

Rob never seemed to have any money, despite the fact that he was earning more than me, and if he asked me to give him some money, then it seemed logical that I should do so. I got round this about eight months before the injunction by opening a secret account so that I never looked like I was flush, and I went without things I really needed, just in case I needed to go it alone.

I asked friends to pray for the situation to become absolutely intolerably dangerous again, or for a very obvious change to occur in Richards's life as the toll on my wellbeing grew more and more serious. My family and my best friends, both locally and very far away, felt that this was the way we should all be praying and that we should be praying that some resolution would occur quickly as they could all see, maybe more than I could, that I couldn't take much more. We all felt the same way over exactly the same weekend, without contacting each other, so then our prayers focused around a resolution, whether it be positive or negative. This can only be God's work because afterwards we all discovered that all were praying for something specific that weekend. I was frightened. I had decided that living in limbo was making me progressively sicker, both physically and mentally, and I couldn't go on much longer without completely breaking. I prayed that God would keep me safe, but I also prayed that if it was going to take a violent physical assault to help me make that final decision, that God would give me the grace and courage to bear it. I had my crisis plan in place, thanks to the outreach service who had also contacted the police and put a history marker on my address and phone number. (A history marker is a note that is flagged up should you dial 999 and shows a history of a particular crime.) I had 'safe words' arranged with fantastic friends who had a spare key and their numbers were programmed into my quick dial phone next to my bed. They knew that if I said certain words they should call the police. Other friends from far away wisely advised me not to creep and crawl all the time but just act normally and see what happened, particularly in view of his 'apology' just four weeks earlier.

I had phoned my minister a few months previously and told him that I really didn't feel I could go on any longer, and for some reason, without even planning the words, I told him that unless something miraculous happened I really couldn't see us being together by Christmas. He was surprised, but supportive and prayed with me over the phone as he had done several times before. I didn't know what was going to happen; I couldn't bear to see the man I loved so much drive off to work one day and know that he wasn't going to be coming home. I knew that I would never be able to do it, and I prayed that God would leave me with no choice.

Chapter Twenty-Three

Earlier in the year I had got in touch with Sharon. Or at least, I had tried to. I had managed to find her on the Internet through her place of work where there had been a mobile number. I knew it would be a work one and therefore not answered, so I left a message simply saying: 'My name is Victoria, and I'm very sorry to bother you if you're not the Sharon I think you are. However, if your surname used to be Court, then I really need your help because my surname is too and I think you'll know what I'm on about.'

Several months prior to this, when Robert was safely away for the weekend, I had tried to find Sharon's phone number in Rob's previous divorce file. I hadn't found it. Rob had shown me this file as soon as we started going out. I am still not sure whether I was so in love that I didn't read it properly, or whether he took it out, but when I found the page with the reasons and examples given I nearly collapsed. It talked about Rob being unable to give any care or love or affection, it said that he lost his temper suddenly and for no apparent reason, and that at times she had been frightened for her physical safety. It also mentioned many other things, like money for example, with which I could identify. I photocopied the file several times, and took one set of the paperwork to a solicitor and told him what was happening. Also, it was about this time that I first phoned the outreach service, just because I wanted to ask them about something legal in the papers that I had found. That was when I discovered that they could meet with me weekly, and they have since transformed my life. Immediately after I spoke to some great friends, and a little while after this

I spoke to my GP, and then to my physio, whose support have played a greater role than they will ever know in my healing process.

I was brave enough to let Rob know that I had found his divorce papers. Again he said it would take a long time to forgive and forget what I had done, it had been so disgraceful (the same as going to see a counsellor). These are, from Robert's own mouth, the two most despicable sins of my marriage. Not once has he stopped to consider why I would need to do either. He screamed and shouted and threatened me that if I ever mentioned Sharon's name again he would not be held responsible for what he would do to me. This time he went white with fury (or maybe fear), not the usual scarlet, and I was glad that I had specifically chosen to tell him five minutes before a friend was due to call.

The day after I left a message on the phone that I guessed may belong to Sharon, my mobile rang, just before work. I asked, 'Are you Sharon who used to be married to Robert?' She said, 'Yes, that's me.' I immediately burst into tears. I knew at that moment that she had been through what I had been through because she said to me, 'Don't worry, I'll be here while you compose yourself, or if you like you can make a coffee and I'll ring you back in ten minutes. I know exactly why you're ringing, so please don't worry, I understand.'

Sharon and I communicate regularly now, and her parents even phone me up too. Sometimes we laugh, sometimes we cry, well, I do anyway! I would like to think that already we have brought an element of healing to each other.

By now there were so many people praying that things would go one way or the other, and that they would do so quickly.

After I was thrown out of the bedroom – this time forever – on our third wedding anniversary, still less than a year ago, I allowed myself to cry, to sob.

I had come home from visiting friends up north especially

for this day, and had bought some Christian CDs at their church. I put the tracks to play on random, and this is what I heard;

"For the joys and for the sorrows,
  the best and worst of times,
For this moment, for tomorrow,
  for all that lies behind;
Fears that crowd around me,
  for the failure of my plans
For the dreams of all I hope to be,
  the truth of what I am:

For this I have Jesus, for this I have Jesus
For this I have Jesus, I have Jesus.

For the tears that flow in secret,
  in the broken times,
for the moments of elation,
  or the troubled mind;
for all the disappointments,
  or the sting of old regrets,
all my prayers and longings
  that seem unanswered yet:

For this I have Jesus, for this I have Jesus
For this I have Jesus, I have Jesus.

For the weakness of my body,
  the burdens of each day,
For the nights of doubt and worry
  when sleep has fled away;
Needing reassurance
  and the will to start again
A steely eyed endurance,
  the strength to fight and win:

For this I have Jesus, for this I have Jesus
For this I have Jesus, I have Jesus."

Graham Kendrick,
© 1994 Make Way Music, www.grahamkendrick.co.uk

Chapter Twenty-Four

21st March 2001

Prayer takes on a completely different look when we experience the loss of someone highly significant in our lives. Grief has a habit of robbing a prayer life. We need to acknowledge our losses, our 'goodbyes', to approach them in a way that can lead eventually to personal growth. God wants to know about the pains in our life, sometimes speaking, sometimes listening, often, in my case, for months and months just calling out 'help' and thanking God that He knows the words I would want to use if I could. Sometimes there is a lot said without any words. One of the amazing things about having a relationship with God is that communication with Him can happen anywhere, any time, any place. It is ironic then, that, often when we need God the most, it is the very time we feel at a loss for words, at the times when we most need to be aware of God's tender compassion and comfort. We often don't have a desire to pray in traumatic times, it doesn't mean that we have lost our faith or that we are being unfaithful to God. I've taken a lot of convincing from a lot of people that depression and feeling as though you are 'going backwards' in the journey of faith are not the same thing - depression affects everything - it doesn't specifically pick on our spiritual life - it affects all parts of us. I feel guilty that I can't read the Bible - but I can't read anything, so God's not sitting up there waiting to pounce! He's the absolute opposite of everything Rob is. His values are the exact opposite. He's not even waiting to judge me when I react in the way that only a traumatised person would - He understands distressed, unclear e-mails, texts, letters, phone calls, without judging and just loving – loving me as though I am the most perfect, worthwhile person on earth. And if I was the only one who had ever done anything wrong, be it the made up imperfections of abuse, or the genuine faults I possess along with everyone else, He would have died for me, just for me – and I have the cheek to call myself worthless! God is not the big judge with a hammer waiting to bop us every time we do something wrong, in the way that the world portrays him. It just means that we are at a bend in the road. I believe that no matter how strong, deep or mature our faith or love of God, there may be moments, sometimes very long moments, in our grieving when we go through the motions of faith only. But sometimes it is in the wintertime of our faith, the seed time before the buds begin to show, where we trust God's healing power can be going on inside us, whilst we move towards spring. God never leaves us, whether our lives be in the spring, summer, autumn or winter. God created us and understands that deep sadness can be part of our human condition.

Surrender walks hand in hand with letting go. To surrender is to give up our own power over something that is holding us down, and giving it to God to deal with. This is not the same as being controlled or not allowing ourselves to be empowered – it is like throwing down a heavy backpack that is weighing us down. Surrender means the challenge of the unknown, the new opportunities of the future. Surrender demands that we trust God within our own lives because He always desires our happiness. He will always be travelling with us, guiding us and sustaining us. To surrender is to be willing to leave our situations in God's hands, as our pacesetter, to let go of the barriers that could potentially harden us or build a high strong wall of isolation around us, as we say, 'I will never get hurt again' (from *Praying our Goodbyes*) – a particularly difficult issue for women who have lived with abuse, as everyone's journey takes a different amount of time. We are all unique and shouldn't compare the length of our journeys - something that has been a big challenge to me, especially with my support from the outreach service, as I have so often felt guilty that I must progress faster in order to 'free up' space for other women, although the workers have never made me feel like this. There are still many traits of victim talk. However, moving on must eventually be part of my journey towards wholeness.

However, this reality of moving on can never happen until we let go of what is holding us to the past. This is one of the reasons I feel that victims of domestic violence have a lengthy journey to travel. If I had a switch labelled 'love' that I could switch on and off at will, I would have switched it off the day I took out the injunction. Or before. But it's not as easy as that. Holding on to things or people saps our inner strength and can mar our vision of where we want to go next and what God wants for us. We must eventually come to a place in our lives where we agree to give up painful memories that harm us, or dashed dreams that discourage us, or heartaching wounds that prevent us from discovering new dreams.

Letting go is not easy. I've written it as though it is and I know all about it. But I don't. Not yet. I can write about it because I can think about it in my mind, although I can't yet often put it into practice - I have not yet travelled far enough in my journey. I don't want to put my husband in a box in the loft and leave him there. I need there to be reminders of him. When he first left, I couldn't sleep without items of his clothing under my pillow. This may sound silly - it does to me now, so I have moved miles - I look at them now and laugh at my memories, but each stage must be reached when I'm ready, although there's also a place for self-control as I travel further along the road in my journey. Just as I think I've learnt to let go of something, I have to relearn it because part of me is choosing to hold on still. I still need to learn that letting go doesn't mean not caring or giving up. Instead we choose to use our energies in other ways and accept that we cannot change the past. All the struggling and grieving of my heart will not bring restoration to my relationship with Rob whilst he is still in deep denial and managing to abuse me via the whole legal settlement. Growth won't happen until I surrender these thoughts. Some of us, and I guess at times I still include myself in this, would rather cling to the present pain than we would face the unknown, no matter how good it may be for me, for us.

However, one thing I do know, and I know with absolute certainty, is that there will come a time when I can regain control of my past, and my past will no longer control me.

That is recovery.

If

If I could give you up
I could
go on with my life
protect my children
get a job
have friends
have a laugh

If I could give you up
I could
leave the dishes in the sink
talk on the phone at night
watch romantic movies on TV
skip dinner
have no beer in the refrigerator
If I could give you up
If.

Breaking Free From Partner Abuse,
Morning Glory Press, 1993. Compiled by Mary Marecek

Now when I read this poem I can change the words to 'when'. Try doing this yourself.

As I write today I am a survivor, although I have a long, long way to travel to full healing.

I phoned a friend from church today – she was just watching the marathon and said it had made her think of me. She had been wondering why during the marathon there were people every now and again who were looking backwards. She was thinking that it would be impossible to win, to fight, to press on, when all the while they were looking back. It was then that she realised that they were the pacesetters. The pacesetters look back and worry (or not!) whilst the competitors look in only one direction – onwards. She said to me, 'Vicky, God is your pacesetter. If anyone is to look back, it's God. You however, must run through your pain barriers in order to win the race. You don't know whether you'll win in record time, or whether you'll be slow, or average, but one thing you do know – if you look forwards, you will win in the end, and if you need to look back, God will do it for you, because He is your pacesetter. Why look back and worry when you could leave that to someone else?' She wasn't trivialising or underestimating my pain and experiences, but what she said was a real blessing to me.

In closing this section of my story, I note two things. One of them I pray that my Rob will remember forever, and that is my last conversation with him on that Monday morning, now nearly four months ago.

21st March 2001

He told me that he had gone into work and they basically told him to pack his bags and leave. He had already had difficulties within the team, and had been given a month's trial at which he had succeeded, but as soon as the pressure was off and things were back to normal he had slipped back into the interpersonal difficulties that have ruled his career, and his life. I don't know where it came from, but when he said he was going up to see his parents for a few days I said that maybe this was a sign that it was time to change a lot of things in his life. He immediately asked, 'Do you mean us?' and I said, 'Yes, I do actually.' He replied that whatever was going to happen should happen amicably, and I replied that yes, this is what I wanted too, but he must not forget that I was still terrified of him. For some reason he asked me if I'd been talking to his mum or anybody, and the words just slipped out, 'No, I've been talking to Sharon …'

I knew then that I would never see my husband as my husband again, and I was the most heart broken and devastated that I have ever been in my life. I think that Rob knew that changes were afoot, but, although what he has done to me and Sharon is criminal, at that moment I loved him as I have never ever, and will never ever, love anyone else again.

I immediately got an ex parte injunction, which means one that the judge granted in Rob's absence, so serious did he consider the risk to my life.

But, before I put the phone down I said to my husband, 'Please just remember one thing, that is that whatever happens I will always love you.'

And although today, as a newborn survivor, I am still terrified when I think of what I have been through, I can still look on Robert as a man, created, as I am, in God's image and pray that somehow, in some way, God will give him the wholeness and renewal that he so badly needs.

And yes, in nine days, the injunction will run out, and to be perfectly honest I don't know whether I am safe or not, but I have learnt that, up to a point, I can choose to stay a victim, or I can choose to be a survivor.

No, it's not as easy as it sounds, and some days I feel that I have no choice, but, as every life begins with God, and will end with Him, I end now with God, for it is true to say that many people who don't claim to be Christians become survivors of domestic violence without God, but I know for a fact that I would not be one of them, so, in the words of a poem I so aptly found:

"Lord, for tomorrow and it's needs, I do not pray,
Stay here with me, my only strength,
Just for today.

So for tomorrow and it's needs, I do not pray,
But keep me, guide me, lead me Lord,
Just for today." E.R. Wilberforce

I am also frequently reminded of those words I found, written in my New Year's prayer this millennium. And no, we still haven't got the finances settled, and it's not all as straightforward as I initially thought it was going to be, and, if I do lose my house with all its adaptations, the stress, right now, on top of the recovery process, it makes me feel as though I will end up losing my job too, as I just can't cope with many more changes just now. But, firstly, I can do everything through Christ, who gives me strength, and, secondly, Rob may be after everything material, in fact, I think that's the only part of me he actually misses, but "naked I came from my mother's womb, naked I will depart. The Lord gave, and the Lord has taken away ..." (Job 1 v 21) at the moment, my idea of marriage, and with it, my hopes, my dreams and everything I have assumed will be mine for life. He may yet take away more materially, if He chooses to, then I'll know it's for the best, because there are bigger and better things waiting for me, maybe not materially, but in love, relationships and dreams.

I pray that whatever happens I will be able to say, with Job in his sufferings, "May the name of the Lord be praised." For it is in Christ, in Christ alone, that I can face whatever He calls me to. He has surrounded me this far, He has never left me; His presence is so close I feel that it couldn't have been as close if my dreams had been fulfilled immediately. God blessed the second half of Job's life more than the first because he trusted in God, and it is in

Christ alone I trust, on Christ alone I lean, and wait for His purposes to be revealed, waiting for a brighter tomorrow where relationships are reciprocal and equal and where I can give and receive, without fear and abuse, as a human being, made in God's image, precious, worthwhile, beautiful to Him, and whole. God loved me so much that He died in my place. How could any individual be anything other than worthwhile – it is impossible to be a Christian and be worthless or useless, even though the abuse has made me feel it so deeply and so often. Marriage was God's idea, and He didn't plan for it to be violent or dominated by Rob.

In church today, I was reminded of my counsellor and my key worker who led me to survival, and to whom this book is dedicated. Our minister was reminding us about an eagle, and how it acts as a mother. An eagle in the Bible is seen as a symbol of strength and long life, a sign of blessing. The eagle is also seen as an image of God, carrying, holding and protecting us. Eagles are also very maternal and have very strong caring instincts. He explained how they feed and nurture their young, day by day, until one day the parent who has nurtured them, given them everything, pushes them, slowly but with determination, out of that nest. How she pushes until they are out and have no choice but to fly. But as soon as their fluttering feathers take their first flight she is underneath, circling around them, waiting, hovering, there to catch them, giving them confidence, and acting as a lifeline, just in case they fall. An eagle will only learn to fly if it's pushed out the nest. There simply is no other way. Then they discover the joy of flight for themselves. This is what God wants for me, and He will be there, always Himself, often also using others, pushing me out further and further, but never leaving me, always there waiting to catch me, so that I'm never alone – not even when I've learnt the joy of flying independently. He will meet my needs, in His time, and one day at a time.

Yours, carried by Him,
Vicky, a survivor.

"Underneath are the everlasting arms." (Deuteronomy 33 v 27)

Part Two
Domestic Violence - The Facts

Domestic violence is an experience that completely alters one's life; not in the same way that 'normal' bereavement, job loss, burglary, and suchlike do. It's in a category all of it's own - like the secret society in which I have felt alone for so long. The pain within a victim's heart can remain long after the broken bones have healed and the scars have faded. There needs to be time for healing; people assume, professionals even tell you that you've 'done the hardest bit', and it seems almost perverse to try and explain that actually adjusting to life without violence can be so difficult. It's just that, for differing amounts of time, every move has been watched, permission has had to be asked, in my case at times even to go to the toilet or make eye contact, that living and fulfilling the most simple of tasks almost require some sort of 'rule book' to follow. People must assume, as I did before, that the adaptation is easy and pleasant - it's not. This week I have pulled my kitchen blind, sometimes below the tiles, sometimes above - I no longer care whether or not they line up exactly with the edge of the tiles - this has been my achievement this week, and it has taken me nearly seventeen months. Yesterday I found the toilet lid up and there had been no visitors in the house, and I was angry, yes angry at myself for breaking a rule. And believe me, I'm not yet ready to do that - I shall make sure I don't do it again for a very long time. These difficulties in adapting to a non-violent life should never be glossed over or underestimated when control has been part of your life for so long.

There seems to be a lot of paradoxes and ironies about domestic violence. One is that the threats that are part of it actually make the victim 'choose' between active violence or colluding with the perpetrator to keep the violence a secret. I now feel embarrassed, stupid even, guilty too, for not seeking help earlier, when in fact it was the abuse itself that prevented me from doing so.

I have mentioned before how people react with alarm when they hear that you have been physically hurt by a partner. However, for many women, myself included, name calling, criticism, casting doubt on sanity (if repeated enough times to an already distressed and traumatised victim), mean that these thoughts actually start to take root, and by this I mean that you actually start to believe it. On top of this, the vast majority of men present a totally different personality to outsiders. Rob, for example, was every woman's dream - always there to help fix things, always refusing to take payment for it, always had time to help (but usually only women, regardless of their age) - when we went to counselling together (something that should never be done) he even 'charmed' the elderly counsellor by taking her bottles of wine and offering to fix her doorbell! Although she was shocked at his treatment of me as a first hand witness, the charm overcame even her, and it really must have done, as I've since found out that counsellors are not allowed to accept gifts. This means that it is easy for other people to think that this violent man is just living in a woman's imagination. Or that she has done something to ask for it. In fact, when I reflect on my own marriage, I was so perfect, so annoyingly perfect, that it makes me sick. I didn't even dare let PMT rear its head when it was just Rob and me! A woman has no one to back her up, the accusations make sense and the cycle is reinforced. I guess I was 'lucky' in that Rob teased and poked me to provoke spasms and humiliated me in public, so that most people's first reaction was 'it was so obvious in retrospect'. But still they weren't usually talking about the physical abuse, the terror that started when the 'happy couple' closed the front door.

On top of this there is fear, anger, disappointment, bitterness, surprise, despair, bewilderment, shame, worry, along with questions like, 'What did I do to warrant that attack?' 'What can I do to improve things?'

The following information is taken from the Women's Aid website, www.womensaid.org.uk, and is protected by copyright to Women's Aid Federation of England (©2006 Women's Aid Federation of England).

"Since abusers typically display different kinds of behaviours in public than they do in their private relations, most people are not usually aware of domestic violence when it is happening in their community. Sometimes it is difficult to believe that a person who behaves so respectfully in public can behave so appallingly with their family. Male privilege operates on an individual and societal level to maintain a system of male dominance where men have power over women and children. However, ultimately responsibility for the violence must lie with the perpetrator of that violence, despite any societal influences that we may draw on in order to understand the context of the behaviour."

We can see, therefore, that abusers abuse just because they can. The reasons that abuse increases or starts as the relationship becomes more committed, is that it leaves the victim in a more vulnerable and confused state, and with less options. The perpetrator also needs to know that his partner is sufficiently committed (or scared), that the likelihood of them being reported is low. The perpetrator, therefore, gets exactly what he wants and the negative cycle is reinforced. Women also have the right to choose, and as difficult as this many seem, they do have the right to stay in the relationship, should they so choose.

However, on a spiritual level it is important to remember that God never condemns a woman for seeking to stop the violence and get protection for herself, in fact, protection from violence is something that is advocated throughout the Bible.

An extremely important point to recognise is that leaving a violent relationship takes an enormous amount of self-confidence and courage - and these are some of the very qualities the abuser is systematically destroying at the same time - this is the major trap in the cycle of domestic violence and something that even the most well-intentioned friends and family may very well not understand. There may be split loyalties because her friends are close to the abuser as well, or they may be afraid to help the victim because of fear that it will backfire on her, or them. I have often thought that this may be one reason why I have so frequently felt misunderstood. In reality, abusers are only 'out to get' one person - their partner - not only during the relationship but after it, sometimes days, sometimes months, sometimes years, sometimes forever; it may, in some cases, feel as though it will never end - but friends and family are safe, because they are still kept in the trap of charm.

I cannot tell you, after years of thinking I was the only person who had experienced these things, these feelings, the only person who had been told she was mad and that the abuse hadn't happened, how amazing it was to find a specific service, one dedicated to dealing with domestic violence; how amazing to find out that nearly all abusers use identical tactics, use denial, use minimisation, call the victims 'mad' - it was as though I had walked onto another planet where, although life couldn't immediately change, I suddenly knew that I was not alone. I really honestly thought I was the only one that this had ever happened to.

Some Common Myths Surrounding Abuse of Women and How to Respond

Myth one: Domestic violence only affects certain social groups

Titles and degrees do not eliminate family violence. A grim

proportion of families hiding this secret are professionals – they can be doctors, lawyers, teachers, solicitors – no sector of society is immune. Victims of domestic violence come from all walks of life. However, it is sometimes easier to hide amongst professionals. I was constantly aware, as fortunately were the police, that throughout my injunction my husband came as close as possible to breaching it without actually doing anything that could get him into trouble. Even as I write today, I feel as though he is still able to abuse me without actually being anywhere near me. Why? Because he is a charmer, and is probably now using it as he has never done before to undermine my friendships, to infiltrate my support network, and to refrain from asking for possessions which I know that he will want at any time. This is almost like my punishment. I know that he will need to contact me through some route, but I don't know when, and that is what unnerves me – like knowing that I had done something 'wrong' when there were visitors in the house, and knowing I was going to pay for it but not knowing exactly when this would happen.

This is because most men who abuse have one thing in common – charm, and as mentioned before, charm and abuse often run alongside each other, or in cycles, cleverly weaving a trap, so that you don't actually realise that you are trapped until you are deeply in it. But all other people see is the charm. They have no need to see the other side. An abuser is often Mr Popular; something that boosts his ego and strengthens the cycle.

We all fall in love with the most lovable (or, in my case, charming) side of our partners, and, like me, invariably remember this charming side that we fell in love with, sometimes to the point where we can fool ourselves that things 'were never really that bad'. It is usual for an abused woman to minimise the bad times, and magnify (in my case to the point of imagination at times) the good times in between. In fact, for me, to come completely out of denial means that Rob will no longer exist, anywhere. And whilst

I, already, am probably 'contained' in the background of his memory as some horrible and distant dream, just as Sharon was, he is still here with me, in every room, at every mealtime, in my nightmares, preventing me from being free in my/our own home whilst preventing me from going out, whilst a few, and fortunately only a few, stand there and gossip about 'poor Rob' and 'everything he's lost'.

The fact that perpetrators of domestic violence often charm others means they are able to get away more easily with behaving abusively because unconsciously they use charm to convince everyone, themselves included, that they're fantastic guys. How could such a charmer be an abuser? This means that abusers can even deny the truth to themselves. In actual fact, there is little difference between charm and manipulation, because both have the ability to bring someone else under control. This is what all abuse boils down to; sometimes obviously, sometimes more subtly.

As mentioned before, men usually only start to abuse once they start to feel a level of commitment in their relationship – before that it's not worth it, and at that point it's too dangerous anyway – they could more easily be spotted. However, once we think that we are in our 'and they lived happily ever after' story and the commitment starts, the charm diminishes because there is simply less, and then no, need. If a man were abusive immediately, then there would be no such thing as domestic violence. Also, you slowly get so used to the moods that can initially be explained away as a 'bad day' and forgive and forget that you eventually find (without realising) that you have become used to responding to his every suggestion and every whim.

A factual insight into domestic violence is that extreme charm is mixed firstly with strange words which make you more and more controlled, interspersed with charm, so that you automatically (whether you're a Christian or not) forgive the perpetrator as 'having had a bad day' etc., until the charm is gradually interspersed with a slight push, all the way until serious assaults are interspersed, and once you're fully trapped, the need to be charming is almost non-existent – except, of course, with everyone else. I'm not just telling you the story of Rob here, this is always the story of domestic violence and how it starts – if a perpetrator showed their true colours initially then there would be no such thing. I remember becoming hysterical the first time Rob punched me; later on, that seemed a ridiculous response because it became my daily life.

Most of us don't know that we are starting out on this dangerous path. By the time we realise, we're trapped. It's only in retrospect in writing my own autobiography that I really realised those early worries, which so easily disappeared in the trap of love. In my case the abuse didn't start with physical actions, and I counted 'just' twenty-nine major physical assaults, as opposed to the average of thirty-five. However, most physical wounds eventually heal, and it's important to remember that non-physical forms of abuse can be just as, if not more, devastating in destroying a woman's confidence and personality by crippling humiliation, belittling and general degradation.

The following information is taken from the Women's Aid website, www.womensaid.org.uk , and is protected by copyright to Women's Aid Federation of England (©2006 Women's Aid Federation of England).

"Women are considerably more likely to experience repeated and severe forms of violence, including sexual violence. The violence they experience is also more likely to have a sustained psychological/emotional impact or result in injury or death. Women may be affected by domestic violence in a number of ways:

- *Loss of opportunity*
- *Isolation from family/friends*
- *Loss of income or work*
- *Homelessness*
- *Emotional/psychological effects such as experiences of*

anxiety, depression, or low self-worth
- *Poor health*
- *Physical injury or ongoing impairment."*

Myth two: It's the woman's fault

Violence is a crime. The woman is the victim, never the criminal. If and when the abuser's actions become public (and this may sometimes be because a woman has been killed by her abuser – two women a week in Britain are killed by their partners) they may claim they have been provoked. Whilst this is rarely true anyhow (most of us spend our time walking on eggshells, giving two hundred per cent, doing whatever we're told without question lest it provoke a battering), even provocation of the worst kind does not justify physical abuse.

Because of the perpetrator's façade to the outside world, often the reaction may be that the woman must be crazy! A charming and abusive man doesn't just convince others that he is the good guy, but he absolutely cannot bear to admit that he has faults himself. The closest that Robert ever came to admitting fault of any kind, abuse aside, was, 'I'm not perfect.'

I was told that I was 'mad' and 'not in my right mind' – even immediately after an attack when I could still be lying on the floor from where I'd been pushed – something particularly hurtful, and something he thought he could get away with because of the medication I was taking to control my muscular spasms. Some men threaten to get their wives institutionalised, say they are concerned about them because they are so depressed, some even convince police that they are afraid for their partner's safety because of their (partner's) state of mind.

Abusers often use social abuse to undermine their partners, humiliating them in front of friends or family, usually quite subtly and cleverly. They know how to make us feel small and insignificant. They know how to make us feel small and put down, so that we feel unsure of ourselves, insecure and weak. One can end up feeling so confused and actively disorientated by the behaviour that we can start to believe ourselves that something is wrong with us. And what's more, many women, myself included, end up needing counselling or psychotherapy as a result of trauma, which, although necessary and no reflection on any historical emotional problems, can reinforce, wrongly of course, that the perpetrator was right. This is why the medical profession also needs specific training, but that's yet another story!

I am still finding out and fighting to remember who I am, or rather who I was, prior to Robert. I feel that I have lost a connection with the real me and don't know who I really am. I felt like I was married to two husbands, and I never knew which one was coming in the front door. Even once I'd established which husband was home, I knew that he could change to the other one at any moment – he was predictably unpredictable, something which was abusive in itself. I found this confusing and frightening, sometimes I knew I had done something wrong (in his eyes) yet I never knew when or how I was going to pay for it. At night-time when I went to bed, I never knew whether I would be ignored, hit, pushed, shouted at, humiliated, or, on those wonderful occasions, loved for just a few precious minutes.

All I knew was that Rob could twist or interpret anything to make it appear, even to me eventually, that I was the cause of his behaviour. I was always told that everything was my fault, as I inadvertently took on more and more responsibility for his behaviour, at first in trying to help him. It was my fault he was tired because I had muscle spasms during the night, it was my fault that he was not growing in his faith, because I was 'such a nightmare', and everything else was my fault pretty much because I was unlovable on the account that I owned two cats! Incidentally, the cats were the only thing that I refused to give away for him from my 'previous life' as he called it.

In common with most abused women I felt guilty and ashamed. I still do when I'm going down a snake's head rather than up the ladder. I feel that I have failed in my relationship; I am only just starting to connect with in my heart and mind together that I was not responsible for Robert's abusive behaviour. I used to spend hours and hours quite literally searching through the recesses of my mind for something I could have done to upset him. When I was brave enough to question he would reply, 'Just think about it! I don't have to justify my actions,' and so I thought about it, and thought about it and thought about it. I was fortunate enough to have friends who had witnessed minor incidents, such as belittling type behaviour, who persuaded me that I wasn't to blame – although to this day I still battle with the concept that I am innocent. Even as I write this now, my stomach is churning, as if it doesn't quite agree with me. I blamed myself for marrying Robert once I could see, in retrospect, that the abuse was there before we were married. I once thought I was stupid for getting into it, and deserved to pay the price by sticking at it forever and ever.

Guilt, along with fear and my strong belief in the sanctity of marriage, made leaving even more difficult. I felt that I shouldn't be putting myself first, that it was acceptable to be exposed to danger at all times, that this was the 'for better or worse' that I had promised before the congregation and before God, despite my church friends and leaders telling me the opposite. I felt I should make sacrifices, and that Robert should come first, no matter what. I felt responsible for him as though he were a little boy; I felt pity for him when I realised that, although he has a generally loving family in most aspects, he never remembered being held as a young child and told, 'I love you.' I wanted to put it right. I wanted to make it better for him. He had taught me that I didn't matter, but he mattered to me, and I felt I should take whatever I had to, to help him become a whole person. It has taken me a long time to realise that we all have choices to make, and that he had made the choice to abuse before and faced the consequences, and he was making the choice to do it again, to me.

Because being abused is so terrible and painful and we can find no rational answers to the question 'why me?', we are so confused that it is usual to forget that it is not us, it is the abuser or the perpetrator's fault. We try to work out what we have done to cause the behaviour, but find no answer or explanation and end up with the assumption that it is because we are so bad that we deserve and warrant this. We have to make sense from chaos, otherwise the world is so senseless and out-of-control, so dangerous and without meaning that we must really be crazy. It is easy to take on feelings of guilt and responsibility, and focus on these, even taking them with us into other parts of our lives, where we feel we are always to blame in every situation where something negative has happened. I still have to watch the tendency to do this - even world famine is my fault and warrants punishment on a bad day!

It is extremely important to remember that it is not your fault. It is not my fault. I now know this in my head, but I still don't always feel it in my heart. In fact, as I write today, I've had one of the worst weeks ever, going back to the stage where I thought I would never return; in fact my goal for this week was to read my own book and believe it! It is also easy eventually to realise it in your head, but to act out in your life and believe it in your heart takes time, and I'm not going to pretend that is always as easy as it sounds when it's written by other people - it is, in fact, three steps forward, two steps back. Unfortunately the healing does not come on an even keel. Sometimes you are certain you can get past the top of the snakes head, and it only takes something, something sometimes very very small indeed, to make you go right back down to the bottom. Even well-intentioned friends can do this without realising. I think I have got unjustly impatient with people who just do not understand, they think they do, they compare it to other situations, whereas in fact their 'help' has been a cause of great distress at times. It is important to realise that we cannot expect everybody to be experts on domestic violence, however much we need this. I certainly hope that some of what I have written will help people to understand a bit more, and that my experiences will not have therefore been in vain.

Myth three: Domestic violence is a private matter that we shouldn't interfere with

Violence is a crime, and that's all there is to it. There are no excuses. Full stop. Most women are unable to fight for their own rights after they have been bullied and harassed. They need help. I needed help. The main place I found this was within specialist agencies, and if you're a woman who is or has been in this situation, a specifically trained organisation will be able to help you too, with their specialist understanding you will not find elsewhere. If you're a woman with children, then the effect on them can be disastrous too. When abuse of women is reduced, child abuse will be reduced automatically too.

Robert repeatedly told me that this was a matter for us, and that we should sort it ourselves. Of course he did, then he could blame me, abuse me and humiliate me as he always had done, whilst digging himself a deeper and deeper hole into the pit of denial. When I initially went for counselling, and eventually told Robert, he told me that it would take him a long time to forgive me for this disgraceful behaviour. I wonder why?!

I started seeing an outreach worker some five months before I finally plucked up the courage to leave. Just seeing someone, and knowing that he didn't know that I was doing this, was, in itself, empowering.

Quite often in our sessions when I was negative (which was most of the time, at least initially) I was asked how I would react or respond to a friend who I knew was going through the same emotions as me. This really made me think, because I knew that I would be giving them the advice that was being given me, so it made me think more seriously about taking the advice myself.

Myth four: Surely there are not that many cases of domestic violence?

Statistics show that in fact one in every four women will experience some form of domestic violence or abuse at some point during their life. It occurs throughout society. Twenty-five per cent of all violent crime is domestic violence. In Britain, two women are killed every week by their partners. Therapeutic reasons aside, I started writing because I was so very frustrated at the complete lack of education and naivety surrounding this topic. The lesson is that no man has the right to keep his partner in line by fear. Statistically, less than half of assaults are reported to the police, but even so, in the UK alone police receive on average one call per minute. Approximately twenty thousand women use refuges every year. This doesn't include the children they bring with them, and on any day somewhere in the region of eight thousand women use some form of specialist support service.

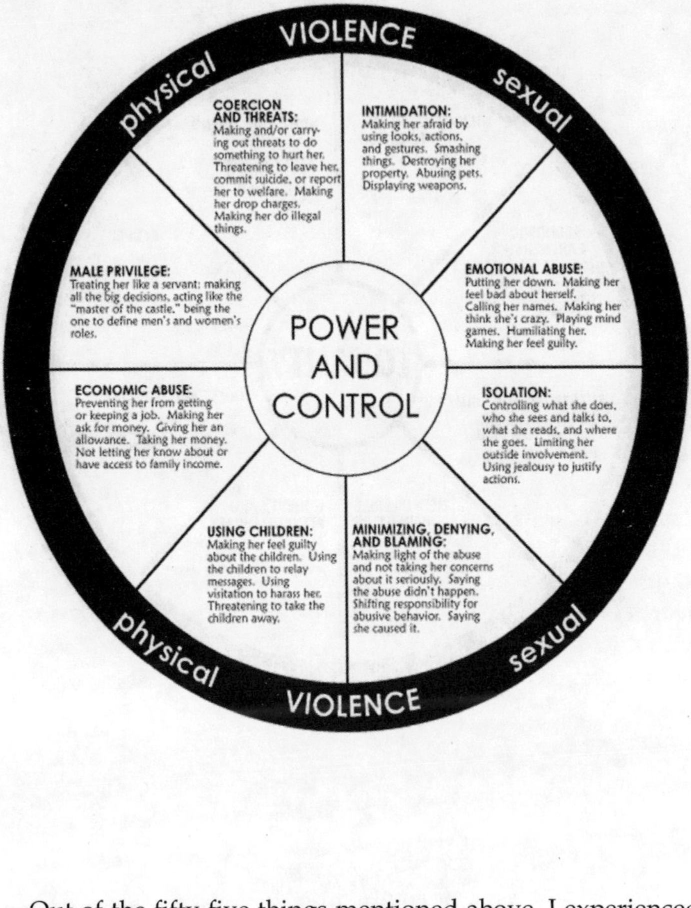

Out of the fifty-five things mentioned above, I experienced forty-two of these on a regular and ongoing basis, and that is bearing in mind that we didn't have children.

When I was first shown this, it came as a shock.

I never knew you were allowed to question your partner.

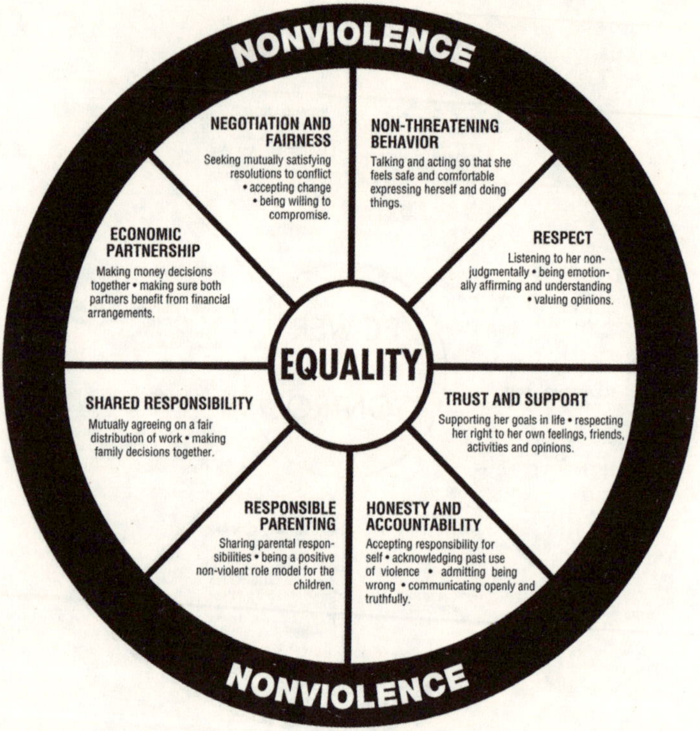

Duluth Wheels (this page and previous page)
Developed by the Domestic Abuse Intervention Project, Duluth, Minnesota, USA

Used with permission from
Oakland County Coordinating Council Against Domestic Violence

Although as far as I know, these wheels were not devised by anyone claiming to have a Christian faith, all the points raised in the equality wheel can be found in the Bible – for example:

- Responsible parenting: Leviticus 19 v 3, "Each of you must respect his mother and father." (Holy Bible)
- Honesty: We need to be truthful with ourselves, with other people and with God. We need to be truthful about past failings and present feelings. The Bible promotes honesty in all relationships, and especially within marriage. Proverbs 24 v 26, "An honest answer is like a kiss on the lips." (Holy Bible)
- Trust: Everyone has the right to live without fear of another person and to be allowed to have contact with friends and family without control or manipulation. 1 John 1 v 18, "There is no fear in love. But perfect love drives out fear, because fear has to do with punishment." (Holy Bible)
- Respect: In a marriage relationship this consists of each partner's need to feel valued, loved and significant being communicated. Song of Songs 1 v 15-16, "How beautiful you are, my darling! Oh how beautiful! Your eyes are doves. How handsome you are, my lover! Oh how charming! And our bed is verdant." (Holy Bible)
- Negotiation versus threats: It is only through discussion and agreement that relationships move forward and if a woman agrees with a man because the only alternative is being abused, then negotiation has definitely not happened.
- Economic partnership: Finances should be used for the benefit of both parties.

(Taken from 'Beaten, battered, bruised and blessed' in *The Church in the 21st Century*, Pastor Joe Hayes)

Myth five: it's the drink that does it/he is mentally ill

Some good friends of mine would love to think that a doctor could just prescribe Robert a pill and then he'd get better. Part of me would like to make that excuse too. Life would then be so much better, and we'd have a future together. Unfortunately, this just sanitises domestic violence. Why had he done it before in his first marriage? He had lost a wife, a home and friends, felt terribly low and I'm sure at times, desperate. So why did he had to do it again? To me? Did he think he would be safer battering me, a Christian who believes in the sanctity of marriage? Did he think it would be easier to prey on someone with a deteriorating disability?

If Robert were ill, I believe he would have been abusive from the start - he couldn't have hidden it until we happened to buy a house together. Most people with mental health problems don't abuse others. Do survivors who are traumatised then start abusing? If men can be careful about times of day, places on the body, and stages of relationships, then there is nothing 'wrong' with their mental health.

If Robert were ill, he couldn't have attacked me, picked up the phone and had a normal conversation for ten minutes, put it down and then carry on where he left off. In all the years I have known my husband, I don't believe he has ever genuinely lost control. It's a choice. It's all about power and control.

Let's face it, there are plenty of men (and woman) who drink too much, often routinely, yet don't harm their partners. It is never the underlying cause of domestic violence, although it is often used as an excuse. Unfortunately, all too often it is also portrayed on TV as being a frequent trigger.

Abusive men usually deny their abuse outright, frequently suggesting that their women are making it up or are crazy. On the occasions when he may admit to something, it will virtually always be minimised, and suggested that his partner is overreacting or exaggerating. Of course, he will also say that it wasn't his fault, that he was provoked.

However, and this is a challenge for us victims too, we too frequently do the same thing, because once we face up to the fact that we are being abused and that it will very rarely, if ever, change, we have to face up to difficult and painful feelings. Of course for most of us we also like to deny it because we are too frightened to do anything else, and the problem, the phantom of fear, is one that very very few people understand.

Once we have admitted that we are living in an abusive situation, we have no choice but to do something about it, so let's face it, it's easier not to. It's not the easiest choice in the world, even some experts like to think – that's why I wanted you to travel with me on the early parts of my journey so that you are informed, and, like me, don't think it's 'only you' having all these feelings. Sometimes I have even said that part of me initially wished I was still living in danger, because it had become my way of life – I didn't account for the ripple effects, the haunting memories, the friends that you're convinced care about you so much that they'll cope, than can't – but for all the negatives there are 'pluses' and they become bigger whilst the negatives get smaller. It's just one step at a time. And when you are able to look at it rationally, ninety-nine per cent of friends do believe you, do stand by you, it's just the way the rejection from the person who's supposed to love you most changes you, and makes the one per cent seem like the end of the world. In the early days, I even went as far as to say that I wished Rob had killed me, because I would have been better off – now I am learning that I always had a lot to give, and that intrinsically I'm the same person – I just need help to rediscover myself.

Even for those of us that don't take action, life will never be the same again, because we know that we are living with an abuser and that things generally get worse not better. In the situation when we are just trying to survive from day to day, it is so often too difficult to think straight. It is so much be easier to justify, excuse and minimise our men's behaviour, and so this is what we do, most of us for a long time, some of us for a very long time, and a few of us until it's too late, ending up as one of the statistics killed each week by a partner.

I survived for nearly four and a half years, using denial as a positive way of surviving, never really thinking I would actually do it but preparing myself just in case I did. I learned to push away everything that was painful. I suffered from daily, severe panic attacks, which stopped the very day I took out the injunction. I also suffered from depression; at times I felt it was really bad, but since the injunction I realised that I couldn't allow myself to sink that low because I had to be on my guard all the time. It has been since the injunction that I have had periods of time that have frightened me intensely, in fact as much as Robert did. We will have a look at some specific help later.

Myth six: The women must be masochists or they would not stay so long

Like most women I felt a failure, and leaving altogether was a total admission of that. After years of being controlled, it was and continues to be a confusing time. Robert has not occupied our/my home for six months, but I still have to check that all the blinds are lined up with the tiles, that each toilet lid is down, that I put things in certain places in the fridge – the list is endless, and when I hung a bag of seeds outside for the birds I felt like a terrible rebel!

But see how things move on, just in the paragraph above I can start to do these things, and yes, they're small things in what seems like a terribly long time, but as I have learnt to jump up and down with enthusiasm when a pupil looks up when their name is called, I must learn more and more to celebrate these tiny achievements of my own, as I would if I were talking to someone else. We often give ourselves a much harder time than we would anyone else – I wouldn't think any woman out there 'pathetic' for following rules eighteen months on, yet I do it to myself – there is a lot to be said for learning to 'love' yourself, to be kind and gentle with yourself as you would be with others.

Also, as has been noted before, it is so easy to magnify the good times so that you only remember them, and minimise, sometimes to the point of exclusion altogether, the bad times. Often we are still very much in love with our husbands or partners, clinging in vain to the false hope that they will change.

Add to that a Christian faith where the sanctity of marriage is foremost, and a marriage that you don't go into with an opt out clause under normal circumstances.

Also, many women feel that they cannot cope or are even more worthless without their partners. Many have nowhere to go. For some it may mean leaving their whole way of life, possibly their home, their friends and all their possessions. This is where refuges and specialist services have a vital role to play.

One of the commonest questions asked is, 'Why does she stay with him?' People who are not in our 'secret club' think it is so easy just to walk out the door and never return. The question in itself implies, once again, that the problem is with the woman – that she should be responsible for ending the abuse. It's like suggesting to someone that they chose to get on a train that was later hijacked.

In an abusive relationship, we have little control over our own lives. I believed, and still do to a certain extent, that Robert needs me, much as he would deny it, although I no longer need him.

The fear factor is also underestimated a great deal in the situations, often with pure fear preventing a woman from leaving. There is a fear that he will come and get you once you have left. You feel as though you will spend the rest of your life looking over your shoulder. Walking out of the door may not necessarily end the nightmare. Sometimes it feels that the only freedom comes from death. In fact, statistics show that the most dangerous time for a woman is at the point of leaving. Two women in the UK are killed each week by domestic violence. If you've never been there it is hard to understand, but there are many reasons women either don't leave, or take so long, and a very important point to remember is that leaving doesn't always stop the violence. Also, they may not work, have anywhere to go, and could have children - add to this the fact that many of us still love our men.

Remember, also, that all decisions have been made for an abused woman, and making them for yourself can seem very daunting.

The following information is taken from the Women's Aid website, www.womensaid.org.uk, and is protected by copyright to Women's Aid Federation of England (©2006 Women's Aid Federation of England).

"Domestic violence can have an enormous effect on your mental health. It is now well accepted that abuse (both in childhood and in adult life) is often the main factor in the development of depression, anxiety and other mental health disorders, and may lead to sleep disturbance, self-harm, suicide and attempted suicide, eating disorders and substance abuse.

Some statistics:

- Abused women are at least three times more likely to experience depression or anxiety disorders than other women.
- Women who use mental health services are much more likely to have experienced domestic violence than women in the general population.
- Seventy per cent of women psychiatric patients and eighty per cent of those in secure settings have histories of physical or sexual abuse.

> Domestic violence has a considerable impact on your health and wellbeing. The results of domestic-violence can be long term and may cause or worsen chronic health problems of various kinds."

Complex chronic post-traumatic stress disorder also has a strong link to domestic violence and is characterised by flashbacks and intrusive thoughts (as if reliving assaults), numbness and a sense of 'not being there' (dissociation), being constantly 'on guard', avoiding people, place and situations that could remind you of the abuse, and many other symptoms. All are normal reactions to stress, with most people showing some signs at some point during their life; but it's if they carry on beyond a few weeks or months that a formal diagnosis is made.

The trap of domestic violence is just so complicated and so 'clever' and is so subtle, until it's too late. Think of an example like this: I meet Rob (or anyone, for the sake of this example), I fall in love. It's normal. It's natural. Eventually I marry. Three weeks afterwards I decide to cook a special dinner, just because I feel like it – I'm in love; again that's normal, it's a great feeling. My husband comes in from work. He doesn't greet me as usual. But that's okay – everyone's entitled to be moody – he probably just had a hard day at the office. I'm entitled to be grumpy every now and again – why shouldn't he? I serve dinner, convinced that my hard efforts will have paid off. He eats a couple of mouthfuls, an expression somewhere between disgust and smugness fills his face. He pushes it away and moves away from the table. 'You don't like it?' I ask. 'It's the most disgusting thing I've ever tasted,' he replies and off he wanders.

Am I going to stand there and say 'Help! Help someone! Dial 999 – I've married an abuser!' Of course not! We are taught from earliest childhood that behaviour is a system of cause and effect – I know it well as a teacher. If a lesson doesn't go to plan, I don't blame the pupils – I blame myself

– I modify the lesson, and try it out when it's improved. No big deal. So I make another dinner the next night, but pay more attention – cause and effect you see. Like the lesson that didn't go so well yesterday but was fine today because I'd changed it, put that much more effort into it. So I make it more tasty. Spend a bit more time. Remember I'm not one now, I'm two. It's exciting! But tonight there's nothing wrong with the meal – it's as though he doesn't realise it's similar to the one he didn't eat the previous night. But tonight I'm making more effort – I'm wearing the little black number he bought me when we were going out. Tonight, he shouts at me and calls me a whore, so I change and then he says I'm letting myself go. Already. And we've only been married three weeks. Again, do I shout for help, and fear that I'm married to an abuser? Of course not. I just worry a bit about what to wear, not because I'm scared, but because I love him and want to please him.

The next time, it's the programme I wanted to watch on TV, but the TV belongs to both of us and he wants control of the remote. And although he's made a fuss about that, he still makes a fuss that I'm calling my mum and not spending time with him. Then there's not enough beer in the fridge, then I've arranged something without consulting him, then it's my fault he's tired and grumpy because I hogged the duvet the last three nights. Soon, all my life's aim is based around pleasing him, walking on eggshells, first just to avoid the moods, but then, almost invariably, to avoid the slap, the punch, the kick. I then have one aim in life – to do better, to rectify this 'cause and effect' I thought I'd learned about, to try harder and then win his favour. The problem is, I never will – you never will. As soon as I get things right, I know the goalposts will change so that I fail. It is absolutely impossible to please an abusive man, because pleasing him robs him of the only thing he craves – control. If this story touches a raw nerve with you and you think that one day you'll get it right – I'm sorry to be hard yet make no apologies for being honest, but you will never get it right, no matter what you do. Because it's not about getting it right - it's about making sure you get it wrong so that he stays in control. Still wonder why it's difficult to leave?

Ending any relationship is painful, but for an abused woman it is much worse. We have to permanently concentrate on the short term and surviving it, without being able to make long term plans.

Myth seven: If women were really bothered by the abuse they would speak up

Obviously a lot of what is written above is also pertinent to this. However, many abused women believe they will be at greater risk if they disclose the abuse. It is only very recently that domestic violence has been taken seriously at all - having spoken to Robert's first wife, she also lived with significant domestic violence, and yet I don't really think she'd thought to label it as such until she came into contact with me, by which time Robert's levels of violence had increased a great deal. However, they had had a friend who was a policeman, to whom she had fled late at night on several occasions in great fear, saying that she'd had an argument, but nothing was ever done about it, she was never asked openly, and he was never challenged.

Self-esteem

I feel I have to write a section on self-esteem or self-worth, because, for me, this is what has been damaged the most. I believe this is true for so many other women too. I needed, and still do, to be told I am an okay person. I need the same sort of reassurance that a young child does when learning to ride a bike, or the reassurance of a patient relearning the first steps after a road accident.

Ironically, many people have reminded me of what I've got to live for, and how I must keep on going to church because it's so important - and not many of them even profess to be Christians! People refer to those who commit suicide as being selfish because of the impact on those left behind. But when you've been abused for five years, and then, as if that's not enough, betrayed (or feel as though you've been betrayed) on top of that - does it not occur to anyone that no one would actually mind if you died? Or, that anyone would actually miss you - a nuisance? Miss the demanding one, the one who goes round and round in circles, seems to get better, then gets worse, with the same issues constantly raising their heads. Sometimes I've wondered how many weeks/months it would take all those who were always going to be here for me to notice if I even moved? Incidentally - a lesson here: never send text messages, or even e-mails about important things - I have had so many of mine misinterpreted and it was no one's fault - and reading them again now I can see why; I was too low and lacking in self-confidence to communicate person to person for a long period of time, especially as it was left to me to initiate any contact with friends as distressed people at their most panic-stricken don't communicate well.

Do people not actually realise that it is possible to sink so low that you think the world would really be better off without you? Or maybe you are so depressed that you actually forget other people exist at all? There is no thought. Just a feeling of sitting at the bottom of a deep, dark, empty well with no way out or up. And you feel so worthless there's no point in anyone even acknowledging your existence.

When God calls himself our Saviour, He isn't referring to one act, performed two thousand years ago. But that does show how far He will go to save us.

A person who needs to be saved is helpless to do anything about it on their own. The situation is quite probably beyond their control. Being saved is to be in a vulnerable position because you feel helpless. But being rescued adds security to life. God is always there, unseen and often, to me recently, unfelt, but there nonetheless. Whatever promises He makes we can be certain He will keep. I have been reminded often of the famous words from Psalm 23: "Even though I walk through the valley of the shadow of death, I will fear no evil, for you are with me." (Holy Bible)

When you are bereaved you don't lose your self-worth. Many spouses know they have been prized, valued, appreciated, treasured. I was criticised, belittled, humiliated, mocked and hurt. Most spouses are grieving, but are honoured by others and have respect for themselves. I was grieving, but was regarded with suspicion by others and felt ashamed of myself.

Shame is to do with who you are - it shows you believe you are a worthless person. People were concerned when I found it difficult to trust them to keep to their word just after the injunction. It is difficult to value yourself highly when the person who is supposed to know and love you the most puts your value at zero. I feel as though I am going through an identity crisis - I want to keep my surname because part of me wants to cling to him still. I've just managed to move my wedding rings onto the opposite hand, although the temptation to move them back again is, at times, overwhelming. After eight months, as the divorce papers threaten to come through the letterbox, I've put a photo of myself and Rob on the front of my mobile phone. Why, after all this time? I guess I just want to remain a 'Mrs'. I've always signed my initial and surname only - suddenly I find myself writing Mrs. Some of my post has suddenly started coming through as 'Ms' - I've never asked for this to happen and I've certainly not written it myself. Some people may think this is very anti-feminist, but I belonged to someone. I may have belonged to an abuser, but I still belonged. I was one of two. It made me feel special- in theory, even if only for social purposes. But I'm not a 'Miss' and can't ever be a 'Miss' again, because I have been a 'Mrs'. I know plenty of people who like to be known as

'Ms' for exactly the opposite reason – they want to be an individual – but to me 'Ms' shouts to the whole world, 'This woman is divorced', or on a particularly sensitive day, 'This woman's been abused.' It also shouts to married women, maybe even to my friends, 'Watch out, she's been married.' I'm just waiting for my male friends to make sure they're never on their own with me, just in case I am waiting there to pounce on them – as though my self-esteem, let alone my morals, would allow me to behave like that.

But there can be healing of self-image. It's a difficult thing, and I'm not there yet. No matter what people tell me, I find it difficult to believe them – I think they're just humouring me. So I end up disagreeing with them, so then they stop doing it, and then it proves my point. But I've realised that I am not allowing anyone to win, myself included, and I'm still stuck in that self-perpetuating cycle. I have 'banned words' during therapy sessions now. I try to ban them the rest of the time too. It doesn't do me any good and it doesn't help other people either. In fact, it probably makes me more like the person Rob pretended I was. So now I'm trying to practice accepting compliments, just smiling instead of screwing my nose up! Maybe, slowly, it will seep into my subconscious. For Jesus says that I am so important that he has my name 'graven on his palms', and that he loves me even more than a mother loves and cares for her newborn baby, and I'm fortunate to have known exceptional love and care on a human level from my mum. And, as a Christian, I have to remember that if I were the only person in the world who had ever fallen short of God's standard of perfection, then Jesus would still willingly have been tortured and died the same death, just for me. That's how special I am! If you can believe that God, who is perfect, loves you, then you can believe that you are worth loving.

So What Next?

No one can help an abused woman until she recognises

what is happening to her. Research shows that men who have abused do not change. As a Christian this has been something that it has been difficult for me to come to terms with, and I want to think about this more in the next section. Unless a man comes out of denial there is no hope. For those who do there is help out there, and there will fortunately always be men who will disprove the rule. However statistically, the reoffending rate is extremely high. In fact, domestic violence has the highest reoffending rate of all crimes.

This is why it is so incredibly difficult for women when you look at everything that they are going through. All the time they are unable to do anything about it they remain in danger, but they are also almost giving their partner a license to continue with his behaviour. Of course, for the woman who leaves, she would have committed the ultimate sin - she will be out from under the regime of power and control, which is what domestic violence is all about. One of my major aims in writing this section is to show just how difficult it is to escape the trap of domestic violence. Every step I took I was told was the hardest step. I am in the hardest step now, living free from violence, without my husband. I am putting myself, at times, through the same things Rob has put me through. Although ultimately we have no choice in order to be safe, please don't feel you have failed when things seem to get more and more difficult initially and you may have been told that they will get easier and easier. They will, but it's not going to happen all at once and it may take a very long, painful and lonely time.

How do you recognise domestic abuse? This is what the Women's Aid website says:

> The following information is taken from the Women's Aid website, www.womensaid.org.uk, and is protected by copyright to Women's Aid Federation of England (©2006 Women's Aid Federation of England).

"Everyone has arguments and everyone disagrees with their partners, family members and others close to them from time to time. And we all do things, at times, that we regret, and which cause unhappiness to those we care about. But if this begins to form a consistent pattern, then it is an indication of domestic violence. The following questions may help you:

- *Has your partner tried to keep you from seeing your friends and family?*
- *Has your partner prevented you from continuing or starting a college course, or from going to work?*
- *Does you partner constantly check up on you or follow you?*
- *Does your partner unjustly accuse you of flirting or of having affairs with others?*
- *Does you partner constantly belittle or humiliate you, or regularly criticise or insult you in front of other people?*
- *Are you ever afraid of your partner?*
- *Have you ever changed you behaviour because you are afraid of what your partner might do or say to you?*
- *Has your partner ever destroyed any of your possessions deliberately?*
- *Has your partner ever hurt or threatened to hurt you or the children?*
- *Has your partner ever kept you short of money so you are unable to buy food and other necessary items for yourself or your children?*
- *Has your partner ever forced you to do something that you really did not want to do?*
- *Has your partner ever tried to prevent you from taking necessary medication; or seeking medical help when you felt you needed it?*
- *Has your partner ever threatened to take your children away or said he would refuse to let you take them with you, or even see them, if you left him?*
- *Has your partner ever forced you to have sex with him*

or other people? Has he made you participate in sexual activities you were uncomfortable with?

- *Has your partner ever tried to prevent you leaving the house?*
- *Does your partner blame his use of alcohol or drugs for his behaviour?*
- *Does your partner control your use of alcohol or drugs (for example, by forcing your intake or by withholding substances)?*

If you answered yes to one or more of the above questions, this indicates that you may be experiencing domestic violence."

As well as the above, if you feel the need to change your behaviour or agree with him, feel you can never get things right, if he constantly rakes up the past, abuses pets, thinks constantly about himself, expecting you to be there for him but fails to show the same care towards you, or if you even begin to think you are 'losing it' (because you're not) – these can also be signs.

A Bit About the Abusive Man

I haven't focused much on what goes on in an abuser's mind in this book because it is their victims we need to be supporting. But I have found it interesting and helpful to try to see the mind through the eyes of a perpetrator, and indeed, this has helped answer many of my questions, such as 'did he plan to abuse me before the relationship even started?' and 'although he can't have loved me in the real way that you and I understand, did he love me in his own way?' It has also helped me understand, as much as I can, power and control through the eyes of an abuser, and has made other things that have happened around me fall into place.

In actual fact, an abusive man needs to seek friends and

allies because apparently it's not as easy as you think to constantly control and intimidate one's partner, especially in these days of changing laws towards perpetrators. A great way to 'win friends and influence people' is to win friends to his side first in order to keep them off the victim's side. Apart from anything else, a perpetrator always thinks he is the martyr or the victim, meaning that he genuinely feels that he deserves allies. This is because the abuser has a completely different value system from the rest of us, and this is where the problem (and the extreme difficulties in ever changing him) lies. It's like expecting us to change our opinions, values and principles and genuinely sticking to these altered values for as long as we live. This is why domestic violence has the highest reoffending rate of all crimes and why, statistically, the likelihood of lasting change is so depressingly low. The fact is "an abuser almost never does anything that he himself considers morally unacceptable. He may hide what he does because he thinks other people would disagree with it, but he feels justified inside. He invariably has a reason that he considers good enough. **In short, an abuser's core problem is that he has a distorted sense of right and wrong."**[1] I have been helped by reading a book called *Why Does He Do That?* by Lundy Bancroft, a man who has given his life to helping well over two thousand abusers in rehabilitation classes. His book is well worth a read if you are interested in the psychology of the abusive man. He gives a telling example whereby he asks his group of men if any of them have felt like calling their mum a 'bitch'. He says that, on average, at least half the men raise their hands. When he asks if anyone has ever called his mum a 'bitch' a gasp of horror goes around the room as if to say 'you can't treat you mother like that!' And we are talking about men who have abused their partners so badly that many lives have

1 From *Why Does He Do That?* (page 35) by Lundy Bancroft, copyright ©2002 by Lundy Bancroft. Used by permission of G. P. Putnam's Sons, a division of Penguin Group (USA) Inc.

been at risk, and many men charged, having served prison sentences or such like. This statement shows us great insight to the mind of an abuser – he is not ill, drunk, a generally violent person – he thinks that his partner (and usually his partner only) should be treated in that way, and that this is justifiable; in other words, in his mind, there is a whole world of beliefs, perceptions and responses that fit together (to him) in a totally logical way; although to us it seems irrational – he just doesn't want us to figure it out. This is one of the reasons for the mind games, and often, the more intelligent an abuser is, the more dangerous and powerful his abuse can be, and the more knots he can tie in his partner's brain.

Abusive Men and Their Allies

Why do men distort their stories so much when seeking support, if they feel that their actions are so justified? In actual fact, an abuser doesn't want to have to explain his worst behaviours because in his heart of hearts he feels these reasons may not be accepted, and he may well lie because also he has convinced himself of his own distortions. It is well known that lie detector tests are usually pointless in the case of ritualistic abuse, so well have they convinced themselves.

An abuser, of course, prefers to have friends completely on their side, but I have never understood why Rob, unlike me, will settle for having some middle ground. Only now does it make sense – and it's exactly the same reason as why domestic violence professionals say that under no circumstances should couples be counselled together – because if a friend takes a middle ground, this means they will consider the problem to be partly hers and partly his, and in the case of abuse, the 'blame' is always one sided – in which case it can't be abuse. I recognise now how much I innocently put myself through both emotionally and psychologically, and at how much risk I put myself in by agreeing to see friends and counsellors with Rob, thinking it would help him. At the time, I could not get anyone to see what the professionals had pointed out - that this was the road to disaster. Something inside had always got extremely agitated when it was referred to as a 'marriage problem' - now I don't just realise I was right, but I understand why. I hope others do too.

> "In reality, to remain neutral is to collude with the abusive man whether or not that is your goal. If you are aware of chronic or severe mistreatment and do not speak out against it, your silence communicates implicitly that you see nothing unacceptable taking place. Abusers interpret silence as approval, or at least as forgiveness. To abused women, meanwhile, the silence means that no one will help - just what her partner wants her to believe.[1]
>
> - When people take a neutral stand between you and your abusive partner, they are in effect supporting him and abandoning you, no matter how much they may claim otherwise.
> - Everyone should be very, very cautious in accepting a man's claim that he has been wrongly accused of abuse or violence. The great majority of allegations of abuse – though not all – are substantially accurate. And an abuser almost never 'seems the type'.
>
> Abused women almost never overlook their partner's humanity. The reverse is true however, he forgets her humanity."[2]

---

1 From *Why Does He Do That?* (page 287) by Lundy Bancroft, copyright ©2002 by Lundy Bancroft. Used by permission of G. P. Putnam's Sons, a division of Penguin Group (USA) Inc.

2 From *Why Does He Do That?* (page 290) by Lundy Bancroft, copyright ©2002 by Lundy Bancroft. Used by permission of G. P. Putnam's Sons, a division of Penguin Group (USA) Inc.

If you only remember one thing, please remember this.

Myths About Abusive Men

1. His previous partner treated him terribly

Lundy Bancroft explains that should your partner *ever* use this as an excuse to mistreat you, you must stop believing anything he says about that relationship, and whether you know or like his ex-partner or not, track her down immediately and talk to her. It is unlikely that you are his first victim. My life started to change once I decided to look for Sharon. Unless action is taken, (and sadly, even if it is), you will probably not be the only or last victim.

2. He cares about me so much. People only show their worst sides to those they really love

Do you lash out at those you love? Is this how you show them how special they are? Most abusive men have more than one close relationship, but guess who they reserve the beatings for? You!

3. He can't show or express his feelings

Wrong! How many times have I said this about Rob! Even now, I can't believe how brainwashed I was by him! He may not be able to show or express his feelings towards me – but guess whose feelings he can? – His own! Again, Lundy Bancroft's work has shown him that in fact the problem is he is far too much in touch with his own and not in touch enough with anyone else's. The whole world revolves around him and his feelings. Abusers tend to express their own feelings more than most men. They have an exaggerated idea of how important their feelings are; they talk about them, act them out till the whole house is full of them. When life is bad for him, then life should stop for everyone else. He expects his discomforts to be 'fixed' for him. His partner's life crises, children's problems etc., nothing else matters; the abusers always try to drive the ball back into their own court because that is familiar and comfortable to them, where their inner world is the only thing that matters.

4. He loses control – he just goes wild

We have seen throughout the book that this is just not the case. However, reading Lundy Bancroft's book about his work with perpetrators gave an extra interesting insight into men who had claimed that before they abused their women they had 'just lost it'. Of many examples the most helpful one to me, partly because it was poignant to my own experiences, was when he asked over two thousand men why they didn't go any further than they did during an attack. One example he gives reads: "You called her a f****** whore, you grabbed the phone out of her hand, and whipped it across the room, and then you gave her a shove and she fell down. There she was at your feet, where it would have been easy to kick in her head. Now you have just finished telling me that you were 'totally out of control' at the time, but you didn't kick her. What stopped you?"

And he then goes on to say, "And the client can *always* give me a reason. E.g. 'I wouldn't want to cause her serious injury' (heard that one), 'I realised one of the children were watching', 'I could kill her if I did that' (heard that one too), and the most frequent of all, 'I wouldn't do that! I would never do something like that to her.'"(And that one ...)[1]

He says that the response that he remembers hearing only twice in fifteen years was, 'I don't know'.

Enough said.

---

1 From *Why Does He Do That?* (page 34) by Lundy Bancroft, copyright ©2002 by Lundy Bancroft. Used by permission of G. P. Putnam's Sons, a division of Penguin Group (USA) Inc.

5. He needs to learn anger management skills or he has a mental illness

It is usual for perpetrators to say when they introduce themselves on a programme, 'I'm here because of my anger'. That's not true. They are there because of their abuse. Men are not abusive because they are angry, they are angry because they are abusive.

When Rob was in the middle of physical violence, his contorted, hateful and bitter face did make him look insane. Yet most men are actually psychologically 'normal'. Their value system, not their psychology, is unhealthy.

Anyhow, mental illness doesn't cause abusiveness any more than alcohol does, as already mentioned.

Occasionally men may be prescribed medication for their abusiveness despite not being classically mentally ill, especially if they are, for example, violent generally and publicly towards others or towards workmates. There can, very occasionally, be an overlapping personality disorder, but this is usually a myth and an excuse. However, there are two main things to watch out for:

- Abusers don't like to be medicated because they are generally too selfish to put up with the side effects. This can then become another tool in psychological abuse.
- No medication yet discovered will turn an abuser into a loving, considerate or appropriate partner. It may just take the edge off the most dangerous behaviours - possibly. But you are only buying time - beware.[1]

6. He has poor self-esteem - he needs building up

Despite Rob's behaviour towards me, top of my agenda was always esteem boosting. I always noticed every detail,

---

1 From *Why Does He Do That?* (page 40) by Lundy Bancroft, copyright ©2002 by Lundy Bancroft. Used by permission of G. P. Putnam's Sons, a division of Penguin Group (USA) Inc.

to the point of what most people would find patronising. I massaged his what I thought was deflated ego constantly, although in all honesty, a great deal of it was in the hopes of diverting another attack. Research shows that you cannot 'manage' an abuser, except for very short periods. My job was probably a hindrance here; I thought I was working towards long term goals whereby I could 'modify' Rob's behaviour towards me. True, it did buy time on occasions, but sometimes when he was grumpy I overdid it, he knew I was scared and then I got into trouble for being scared. Without realising it, I was making the problem worse. "An abusive man never gets to the point where he is satisfied, where he has been given enough. Rather he gets used to the luxurious treatment and escalates his demands."[1] An abusive man gets a lot of privileges whereby his behaviour becomes rewarding - he gets every demand met, he gets his way all the time, his partner does everything in her power all the time to keep him sweet whatever the cost to herself so that he doesn't explode and then, on top of all that, he is praised for being such a wonderful person!

I have written a section on self-esteem in this book because it's the thing that affected me the worst - I guess I'm not alone in this. Think about how your self-esteem has plummeted - probably. Have you turned into the sort of abusive person described above?!

7. He has poor communication and conflict resolution skills

Incidentally, Rob used to blame me for his lack of promotion at work and for the problems he had there interacting with staff. However, research has also shown that there are no known cases where a man's behaviour at home has improved as a result of an improved job situation.

---

1 From *Why Does He Do That?* (page 47) by Lundy Bancroft, copyright ©2002 by Lundy Bancroft. Used by permission of G. P. Putnam's Sons, a division of Penguin Group (USA) Inc.

I made poor communication skills an excuse for Rob for a long time. I spent hours on the internet looking up all types of semantic-pragmatic disorders, which again diverted me and made me pity him because of my job. However, Lundy Bancroft states, "An abusive man is not *unable* to resolve conflicts non-abusively; he is *unwilling* to do so. The skill deficits of abusers have been the subject of a number of research studies, and the results led to the following conclusion: Abusers have normal abilities in conflict resolution, communication and assertiveness *when they choose to use them.* They typically get through tense situations at work without threatening anyone [this is where I do feel like I want to excuse Rob as having a problem because he didn't manage to as a rule, although he was just 'difficult' not abusive ... and this was mainly because he was so busy thinking about his own needs] but they don't *want* to handle these kinds of issues non-abusively when it comes to their partners. You can equip an abuser with the most innovative, new age skills for expressing his deep emotions, listening actively, and using win-win bargaining, and then he will go home and continue abusing."[1]

8. Abuse is as bad for the man as it is for the woman

Abusers get over the pain of abuse incidents far, far faster than their partners. Whilst it's obviously not a healthy lifestyle for a man, they generally do not suffer (despite portraying themselves as the victim) emotional, physical or psychological pain, loss of freedom or self-blame. These, instead, are left to the innocent victims to carry around and deal with for years. Unlike alcoholics or drug addicts, abusers don't tend to hit 'rock bottom' even if facing custodial sentences for their assaults. For decades sometimes, men remain healthy, have

1 From *Why Does He Do That?* (page 44) by Lundy Bancroft, copyright ©2002 by Lundy Bancroft. Used by permission of G. P. Putnam's Sons, a division of Penguin Group (USA) Inc.

friendships, and maintain careers because in many ways they actually benefit from their controlling behaviours. "An abuser can usually outperform his victim on psychological tests, such as the ones that may be required during custody disputes because he isn't the one who has been traumatised through years of psychological or physical assault."[1]

It should also be noted that men who are abusive can fool everyone but the most specifically trained counsellors or therapists. I have found this to be true during routine counselling. Any man who admits or is forced into receiving help needs specially dedicated and trained domestic violence staff. Rob was even able to charm his counsellor so that she believed he was making progress. I have heard him say to her how thankful he is he found her, how she could change his life, and how he could start to see he was completely to blame, yet when he came home, those were the times I was most at risk. This is also a factor in Lundy Bancroft's book. It sounds a harsh and unforgiving thing to say - it is not - it is a life preserving tactic - never believe what a man says until he has proved himself over years and years and has made himself accountable over a very long term to a trained domestic violence counsellor.

Back to Us ...

It is really important that a woman speaks to someone about what she is going through. It is always possible to speak to national domestic violence organisations confidentially and you may be able to meet locally and at mutually convenient times and places. I actually found it quite empowering to know that I was speaking to these people and that my husband didn't know! I actually only rang initially for some

---

1 From *Why Does He Do That?* (page 47) by Lundy Bancroft, copyright ©2002 by Lundy Bancroft. Used by permission of G. P. Putnam's Sons, a division of Penguin Group (USA) Inc.

legal advice, with no idea that I could have the level of support I have had, and retrospectively I wish I had met them years ago. I have had anxieties around meetings even with professionals, because I always want to rate my 'abuse' against other people's, to make sure that I am not wasting their time. But of course they're used to that, because so many of us feel exactly the same. They will tell you that when you are in the room with them you're the only person that matters. I still want to know the answers to questions like: 'Am my using the service more than other people? Less than other people? Am I healing quicker or slower than other people?' Basically, what I still want to know is: 'Am I a waste of time?' Not that anyone has ever made me feel like that, quite the opposite!

Once you are talking to someone, you might find, like me, that your whole attitude and approach changes. You now want to tell a friend that you know will keep it confidential, or a friend who has noticed suspicious behaviour in the past. I found that once I had told a couple of people and they were not surprised (albeit shocked and upset to have it confirmed), I then wanted to tell other people, and then others. Soon I felt much braver within myself, simply because I had a secret support network around me to whom I could talk and stay sane. Likewise, it is so important to get injuries or assaults, even if 'just' verbal, noted by the medical profession, and to take your own photos of injuries and records of assaults and keep them at a friend's house. It is likely that your GP will encourage you to go to the police, but they can't make you – it means that you can stay should you chose to, but if you leave there will be a professional record which makes evidence much easier to collect. Also ask friends to note dates and times if they witness things. It was tiny little things like that that made my case so much more difficult to 'prove', even though the police always believed me. They need black and white evidence, they can't just go on what they feel about your behaviour and that of the perpetrator.

My outreach workers helped me to do some important things, most of which I had already done by the time I contacted them; they then helped me to form a proper crisis plan, which is very important.

The following is a seemingly obvious but an important list of things that I had done:

- Ironically, I had kept some incidents dated and recorded on a floppy disk, (even though I 'was not being abused'!?) which was backed up and copies were kept at work and with friends. I wish I'd had more, but at the time we shared a laptop so I could only record stuff whilst Rob was working many miles away, as handwriting is very difficult for me.
- Numbers were programmed into the speed dial on my mobile and all phones in the house. I learned how to press the correct numbers whilst the phone was in my pocket, without looking.
- I had 'safe' words which I would say to friends on the phone to indicate if I was okay or not.
- I had places to stay overnight if I had to, and a list of important telephone numbers.
- I had a car with many secret underfloor storage spaces which were very useful for the odd pack of underwear and box of tablets - anyone else finding this would have wondered what on earth I was up to!
- An overnight bag was packed (in retrospect, this would have been better left at a friend's house, but it went unnoticed in my boot for many months).
- I used a different delivery address for correspondence and books/information on domestic violence.
- I had a lifeline installed because of my disability, and they were later made aware of the additional circumstances by the outreach service.
- I had a list of information including financial stuff and house information copied and left in safe places.
- I carried important documentation on me at all times.

- Someone explained to me how to get rid of pages on the internet which I had viewed.
- I always carried my car and house keys and mobile in my pocket.
- I learned to sit or stand nearer to any exit in any room.
- I wanted to, but didn't tell my neighbours about what was happening. I told them after the injunction and they are always on the lookout and have spare keys.
- I avoided the bathroom and kitchen when Rob started to look 'wound up'.
- I left spare keys with as many trusted people as possible.
- I kept a spare mobile battery, fully charged at all times, and a charger in the car, plus change for a public telephone box.
- When I was feeling brave, I kept a dictaphone in my pocket to record incidents. This was suggested by a professional (not a specialist domestic violence worker) and was probably risky.
- I visited a solicitor used specifically but the outreach service so that I knew my options and my paperwork were all prepared. I did this because I never wanted to leave and knew if it came to this I would lack coherence and be very upset, so it was helpful to know it was all ready but I didn't have to use it.
- I informed my boss, who in turn informed the secretaries and all those who potentially let people in or out.
- I arranged with my mum that I would give her three rings at a set time every morning to make sure I was okay.
- All locks were changed and shock alarms/sirens fitted on the day of the injunction. This was done by a locksmith who works for the police.
- I had a brighter security light with motion sensor installed, plus an entry system with handset so I know who is at the front door before opening it.
- I kept the injunction papers on me at all times.
- I changed the times I went places as far as possible, and

tried to vary my routine, and started using a different supermarket.

It is also really important to go to the right person. I involved some people for whom it was out of their depth – I did this rather than go to the police, and if I lived my life again, God forbid, I would now go straight to the police or the doctors' with any injuries in order to press charges at a later date. Just because people are loving and understanding does not mean that they are experts, and how a woman is treated initially can determine whether she continues to seek help or continues to live in an abusive relationship. Fortunately, I was seeking help from both specialist services and counsellors at the same time as other people, so this did not matter so much to me.

I spoke to my doctor about my home situation just a couple of months before taking out the injunction. I thought he had realised this before as he had asked me some outright questions to which I had lied, but at the same time I had covered them up so very well and appeared to be blocking every suggestion he made which could help me. This was because my husband was not allowing me to have any adaptations to the house, or use my wheelchair in public because he didn't like the way I looked with these special aids. He actually said that he would prefer that I was uncomfortable, or that I risked tripping, rather than put the price of the house down because it looked like it was a special-needs house. At the time my doctor said that I was colluding with my husband if I was not prepared to do anything about it. Fortunately, by the time I told him, I had had enough input from trained people to understand that this was his way of caring, rather than any direct criticism. However, it is really important that a woman is treated in the right way from the first second she opens up. If not, she may never go for help again and maybe destined to a violent life forever.

It is really important that no one, whether well-meaning

friends, relatives or professionals, force a woman into leaving because this is just swapping one form of control for another, and a target for all abused women is to get their life back, with support, but encouraging empowerment throughout. Only the woman can be guided into leaving in her own time, and this is a process. I believe the process starts when the violence is acknowledged and the end result is the woman actually leaving. I left inside many months before I left in reality. My guess would be that this is quite normal. Leaving is never a single act in a situation like this. For me there were several turning points before I finally left, and I guess there are for most women, but each will have a slightly different story. Don't be surprised at the jumble of emotions – in my experience I think I have confused many friends by sharing the strange mixture of emotions with them. Other people cannot possibly understand the anger, the sadness, the guilt, the blame, the shame, the intense fear and the intense love all mixed up together. So even less will they understand those days when you really, really want to call him, when you really, really want to ask him back when you really, really can't remember or choose not remember the bad times. Sometimes, I have decided, it is best to keep these conversations and these thoughts for those people who understand, like trained staff. And no, the problems don't go away with your partner, sometimes things get even harder initially, but remember that you are embarking on a new life, a life free from violence, a life where you can be treated as an equal in new and interdependent relationships.

A woman's needs must be taken seriously and need addressed immediately by whoever she chooses to go to, because this initial visit could 'make or break' the rest of her life. If the person is too busy, she might never bother again and be pushed back into the situation she is trying to leave. She may even be a murder statistic. It is important that professionals do not suggest talking to both parties as, although unintended, this implies to both that the woman has somehow played a part in the violence. Instead, she is simply trying to break free. One of the letters I received from the CPS from a so-called 'expert' in domestic violence stated that is was undermining that I took so long to report the crime and then opened up, bit by bit. And that was an expert! At the time I was told it was unusual nowadays for women's cases not to go to court, but I have since met up with a group of survivors and none of them have had any notice taken of them by the CPS, even though, in one case, the police had several 999 calls and witnessed an attack. We have become so used to minimising our own pain and excusing our partners, that women nearly always either omit certain events or simply become 'numb' to them because they have become part of daily life.

It is well known by those high up in domestic violence organisations, many of whom have written about it, that often women are so quiet and say so little when they initially seek help that is appears a mystery that they have even asked for any support. Rebuilding self-esteem and confidence enough for a woman to talk through all that has happened may take a long time and a lot of patience on behalf of the workers too. I know that during outreach or therapy sessions I hide behind the masks that I used in my marriage; I don't want to, but it feels safe and I've never known anyone long enough to feel safe yet to remove them. It can take months. The legal 'expert' system has an awful lot to learn.

I have found that I have needed more professional support since leaving than I did whilst staying. For me, and no doubt many other women, it was too dangerous to drop my guard whilst in the relationship, leaving five years' worth of pent up emotions to come pouring out afterwards. It is important that no one tries to speed up this process. I have been tempted often to leave support behind, as I feel better for a short time without support. But I know that this is sweeping the problem under the carpet, and that sleeping the day away, or working the day away won't 'disappear' the problem; it needs to be faced however painful it may be.

Many women have been so caught up in worlds of guilt and insecurity that expressing real feelings become extremely difficult. It is important to start to learn to acknowledge them, to get in touch with them, however difficult it may be. I was not allowed to express any real, meaningful emotions for nearly five years, so getting in touch with them now is difficult - now that I have learned to cry again I feel that I am doing something strange and abnormal, I remember all the awful things Robert used to say about me when the abuse first started and I would initially cry, until I learnt it was all over quicker if I didn't. I managed to push emotions out by being very busy, sorting paperwork, packing his things, throwing myself into work with an enthusiasm not noted for a while, agreeing to take on all sorts of things I was really too tired to do; because I was busy doing practical things, I could push the real deep emotions to the side - I could put them on hold.

I remember when suddenly I'd done all the practical things I could do, and there was nothing left except my thoughts - that was when I felt low, and needed help to express them. Whilst all women suffer to some degree or another from post-traumatic stress after leaving a relationship which has involved physical violence, there can also be extreme positive emotions - I have never seriously questioned the correctness of my decision - and for me, I started sleeping for the first time in years because I knew I was safe. The panic attacks too, in my case, stopped as though someone had flicked a switch.

You will need loving support networks around you, and this is not always possible, and not always the case. Or even the best friends come and go according to their own situations and ability (or otherwise) to handle the pressure. The Samaritans can help, as can the police, and 24, and other 'out of hours' helplines can give you the phone numbers of various options when life seems especially bleak, usually at night when it's too late to access friends.

What I found so amazing about dealing with a specialist organisation was that for every confusing emotion I expressed, there was someone there to say, 'Oh, lots of women say that.' I cannot stress enough how encouraging that is when you think, and have probably been told, that you are the only one. Sometimes this is enough to stop the downwards spiral of false guilt.

I was always confused that Robert quickly eradicated the very parts of me that he had fallen in love with. I found that one of the most confusing things. Maybe, once he had me all the time, those very qualities threatened him, so it made him undermine me, making me feel totally worthless and unloveable, often blaming the qualities which he had fallen for in the first place.

It is important to take one day at a time. I didn't feel like a coper. I still don't always. But I must be, otherwise I couldn't have lived and coped for so long in such a situation. And always try to remember, above all else (and I know from experience that this easier said than done sometimes) that you are the <u>innocent victim.</u> No one can change your partner – the only person who can change him is him.

Please remember that you are not alone, you are part of a wider scenario. I can tell you, not as a trained professional, but as a one time victim, and a newborn survivor not yet quite ready to leave that nest, that it is possible to break away from abuse and build a new life, a life free from violence, power and control. There are days when I still feel like a victim, but I know I have been given the skills to cope and that, up to a certain point, I can now choose to be a victim or choose to be a survivor.

Some of us may have bigger obstacles in our way than others – I am fortunate to be in my own home still at present, and to have a faith without which I feel I could not have survived. Some of you may think I've had it comparatively easy. Maybe in this area I have. However I still have to carry around the physical pain of a degenerative disease, made worse forever by four and a half years of abuse. I have yet to find out whether all my future plans have been ruined permanently, or just put on hold.

But I do know, deep, deep down in my heart where sometimes not even I can reach, there is a seed waiting to grow and flourish until it becomes beautiful again. I end this section with a short piece of writing given to me by my first outreach worker. I don't know whether it was just for me or whether it's something they give to everyone but I like to think it is special, and just for me, and I am sharing it with you now, because you are special too.

> "When we plant a rose seed in the soil, we notice that it is small, but we do not criticise it as 'rootless and stemless'. We treat it as the seed, giving it the water and nourishment required of the seed. When it first shoots up out of the earth, we don't condemn it as immature and underdeveloped; nor do we criticise the buds for not being open when they appear. We stand in wonder at the process taking place and give the plant the care it needs at each stage of its development. The rose is a rose from the time it is a seed to the time it dies. Within it, at all times, it contains its whole potential. It seems to be constantly in the process of change; yet at each stage, at each moment, it is perfectly all right as it is." Anon

Part Three
God and the Church

The pathway to emotional healing and freedom to enjoy your life is not necessarily easy but it is definitely better than staying in the prison of the victim. No experience in life is ever wasted or in vain if you give all your anxieties to God. Even a life that seems full of shattered dreams can be reshaped by God who can make all the broken pieces of the past into something beautiful. I have at times, felt overwhelmed by my life violated through abuse. So many times I have reached the point where I have said 'I can't handle this'. I feel overwhelmed by the problems that basically come from a broken heart. Often it's felt so broken that I felt I could physically die of a broken heart. I need inner support to keep me from being overwhelmed constantly by outward circumstances too. I know that only God can gather up my shattered dreams and mould me into the image of Christ. For all I know, to do that He may need to crush the few pieces I have left into fine clay, put me back on His potter's wheel and make something more beautiful in His eyes than was there originally. He is more than capable of designing something miraculous from the little I have left.

Even as Christians, we are not always delivered from distress at the precise moment we call on God. Sometimes we must endure for a while and be patient and continue in faith, knowing that God's timing is always perfect, knowing that we often only understand things in retrospect. However we know that we have been created by God to be happy and feel good about ourselves. If you can believe that God, who is perfect, loves you, then you can believe that you too are worth loving. Romans 8 v 35 (Holy Bible) says: "Who shall separate us from the love of Christ? Shall trouble or hardship or persecution or famine or nakedness or danger or sword? No, in all these things we are more than conquerors through Him who loved us. For I am convinced that neither death nor life, neither angels nor demons, neither the present nor the future, nor any powers, neither height nor depth, nor anything else in all creation, will be able to separate us from the love of God that is in Christ Jesus our Lord."

Before starting this section, I feel there are a few points I need to make. Maybe some of you are reading this book for the first two sections only, and only reading this bit simply because it's here. True Christians do not believe they're perfect. We are no different from anyone else. We are no better than anyone else. We are simply human beings who have realised our imperfections, have admitted them, and have passed them over to God to deal with, as the only example of perfection and pure, untainted love, strength, justice and reliability in our universe. When we pass our sinful natures over to Him, we then live in the knowledge that He looks upon us as perfect, as His children, even though we are still fallible humans.

This means that we still make mistakes, we are still wrong at times, we are just like everyone else except that we have a saviour who is there for anyone who is prepared to call on Him.

This also means, because we are fallible, we all make mistakes, whatever our position in the Church or otherwise. During the majority of this process, I have been very fortunate to be loved, phoned, visited, and my practical actions not just supported, but encouraged.

Educating people while you are hurt is difficult, if not impossible. Reconciliations do happen in 'normal' marriage break-ups. They very occasionally happen in cases of domestic violence too, although the rehabilitation rate for perpetrators, even confessing Christians, is depressingly low. People say that God can do the impossible. I believe this. It's supposed to be comforting, but it's like pouring salt on a raw wound. It's the same as trying to resurrect something that's already died. Remember that an abused woman, in particular, is so vulnerable, because she may be fighting the temptation to return to an abusive husband, as I have done so many times, so comments like this can be actively dangerous.

I would be very surprised if anyone could come up with anything that I haven't thought over, prayed over, cried over, screamed over time and time again. It's probably the same for all of us who have been abused. Please give us support, love and acceptance. Reassure us a lot that we are okay people – remember the person that was supposed to love and know us the best has spent years (and there are so many women out there who are abused over a much longer time period), in my case on a daily basis, telling us that we are not. I have felt that I'm everything but an okay person and that everything about me physically, emotionally and my personality is unlovable and unattractive. My interests and hobbies are 'pathetic'. (That's a banned word now!) I'm not disabled, I'm a 'defect' who 'uses her disability to her own advantage'. Add to that the fact that I have upset more people through my depression in the months since the injunction, than I have in the rest of my life put together and you may start understand how I, how we, feel about ourselves. I can honestly say that I have never had a serious argument, been deliberately rude, 'fallen out' or had unrealistic expectations of people in all my life. Now I am doing it but I still need understanding and acceptance. Otherwise I am scared of turning into the person that Rob made me out to be – a person that, even at my lowest, I know I'm definitely not.

Add to this all the things you have read in the previous two sections, and I pray that anyone who falls into any of these categories may understand the complete and utter devastation that can potentially be caused by the best intentioned Christians, who are simply uneducated in domestic violence, or who may have that little bit of pride or sin, which may wash over anyone else, yet could cause an abused woman to be either another murder or suicide statistic.

We must always bear in mind that where man's word conflicts with the words of the Bible, it is the Bible to which we must listen since man is fallible and the Bible is not. I have been very blessed to have been loved and supported in a close Christian network, but it is very important to remember at all times that our trust is in an infallible God, and not in fallible humans. Many of my friends have referred to my church as hypocritical. This is always a difficult one to answer when they are standing so closely by you and see the distress caused by Christian peers at times. But without going along to a church, and understanding it, it's not possible to judge. I know of no one at church who claims to be better than anyone else. That's not what true Christianity is all about; it's actually about recognising that you're far from perfect and asking for help. Hypocritical doesn't come into it, unless you meet someone who claims to be perfect, and I've not met anyone in any church I've been to who has done yet. But that never excuses us from not being role models.

There is a place for forgiveness. Forgiveness for those who have not understood, as well as forgiveness for the abusers. We have a difficult path to tread when we are already victims, the innocent victims, then faced with additional difficulties, even betrayal, albeit unintentional. Try to pray for those who have betrayed you, and by this, I do not necessarily just mean your abuser, I mean people who should, but don't, understand. Sit quietly and try to imagine Jesus being spat at at the foot of the cross, preparing to die for the sins of all of us, even for those who have helped us, yet don't realise how much He has done for us. Feel the strengths of God's love flowing through your being, picture

His hand in yours as you begin to pour out your heart to Him.

Here is a prayer of one who has been betrayed by others, from the book *Praying Our Goodbyes.*

> *"Keep my heart open to loving others and to being loved by them, O God. Do not allow me to close off my life because of the scars of this painful rejection, lead me into peace of heart. Help me to believe in my own goodness, so much so that I can reach out to others with confidence and receive their affection with trust. I pray for all those who have been brutally and harshly betrayed ... and I pray for the one(s) who has rejected me. Jesus, you continued to be a loving person even though you had been so painfully treated, please help me to be a loving person too. Amen."*

In her book, Joyce Rupp also explains that one of the reasons that it is so easy to fail in knowing God as deeply as we could is that we do not always let Him carry things for us in reality rather than just in study. We can walk through fire with Him yet not be burned, we can walk with Him and not be crushed under a load because He can carry it for us. Indeed, Christ can carry our sins, our anxieties and burdens. He can carry our anxieties about being useless, being weak, being worthless, making decisions and being afflicted. He will also carry the cause of justice for us because in almost every relationship in life, whether we are abused or not, we will be treated unjustly at some point. Jesus never called us to a fair fight, but he will finally settle accounts for us, and in the end the Christian life is the life of being carried from beginning to end. There is a well-known piece of writing which encourages me every day; and although I'm sure you will know already I want to remind you of it here.

> *"One night a man had a dream. He dreamed he was walking along the beach with the Lord. Across the sky flashed scenes from his life. For each scene, he noticed two sets of footprints*

in the sand; one belonged to him and the other to the Lord. When the last scene of his life flashed before him, he looked back at the footprints in the sand. He noticed that many times along the path of his life there was only one set of footprints. He also noticed that it happened at the very lowest and saddest times in his life. This really bothered him and he questioned the Lord about it:. 'Lord, you said that once I decided should follow you, you would walk with me all the way. But I have noticed that during the most troublesome times in my life, there is only one set of footprints. I don't understand why when I needed you the most you would leave me.' The Lord replied, 'my precious, precious child, I love you and I would never leave you. During your times of trial and suffering, when you see only one set of footprints, it was then that I carried you.'" (Mary Stevenson)

Remember that whatever you're going through, there is nowhere so deep, so dark, so lonely or so frightening that God won't be there too.

So, what does the Church really believe about domestic violence?

Domestic violence isn't a new problem but it is the new problem for Christian leaders who are being called upon more and more to face the challenge of this issue that has previously been thought of as 'private'- and something in which we must not intervene as it is between two people and two people only.

Remember that, unlike arguments which can be positive and have productive outcomes, domestic violence is not a case of arguments (I used to say that I would be the happiest woman alive the day that Rob and I had a 'proper' argument), it is the abuse of male physical power to dominate and control.

There are only so many pieces a victim can be broken into before a whole life is shattered beyond repair. I firmly believe that in my life at least, only God can provide the glue to rebuild and restore a broken body, mind and spirit.

I am sure there are many theological arguments that we could get into regarding abuse, but the issue here is all about rebuilding broken lives rather than debates in theology. All we really need to believe is that the love of God is pure and perfect and that God hates violence of any kind, whether it be rioting, fighting, bullying, adultery, child abuse or domestic violence. There is only one difference between the things in this list, and that is that they are all condemned publicly with the exception of domestic violence. What makes this all the more ironic is that a home should be the place where each of us feels safest to be ourselves, both safe and protected. By ignoring, or not mentioning it, it indicates that it is an issue about which the Church feels they can evade all responsibility. Domestic violence is not a private affair - this is exactly the excuse that perpetrators themselves use. Jesus came to protect the weak and vulnerable, and the Church has a responsibility to do the same. It is true that the Bible does portray women as physically vulnerable and in need of protection from the overbearing physical dominance of man, with an emphasis on consideration, respect and love governing all relationships, not just Christian, but all relationships. God never intended anyone to live in a hostile environment, so whether violence in the home is open or secret then it is always totally unacceptable in God's eyes.

A personal opinion is that we must all challenge our own beliefs about abuse if we are to be able to deal with it effectively. Some of the myths mentioned in the second section of this book apply equally to church leaders as they will do to victims, perpetrators, families, professionals and even medical staff. The full extent of domestic abuse is difficult to communicate as it is still predominantly a hidden crime with most women choosing not to report it.

The Church and Christian victims have more myths and misconceptions to face because of the verses in scripture to do with submission which have resulted in many women seeing abuse as 'just another cross to bear' which of course is completely unbiblical. Verses in the Bible to do with submission, whilst referring to different roles, are always about equality in relationships, with the concept of one person controlling another being a complete misinterpretation of the Bible. 'Christian' perpetrators often use a twisted teaching of headship and submission to abuse their partners or wives. A Christian wife, already ground down by constant abuse, is in danger of thinking she must comply with her husband's wishes and that this is suffering in the same way as Jesus did – a particularly dangerous misconception. It is important to remember that Jesus suffered for our wellbeing, he wasn't giving in to the evil actions of his enemies but rather submitting to God for His glory and honour.

As a Christian woman myself, I was constantly believing, as I still do, that the power of prayer can change my abuser. However, what I have now learned is that God is in control of Rob's life, not me, and that I didn't have to leave myself in a position of danger in order to see him changed. God can work miracles, but He doesn't need or expect me to live my life in danger whilst I wait to see whether or not this will happen. For a long time I believed that if I persevered and showed Rob the love of Jesus, my own actions would save him. I also believed that if I told anyone that it would be a bad 'witness', something that kept me in the relationship significantly longer than I may have been otherwise. This, of course, was reinforced by Rob, who told me constantly that I was a poor example to him, and blamed me for him not growing in faith to the point where I was brainwashed. In the Bible, Jesus would not allow a prostitute to be stoned, so he is hardly going to condone domestic violence, or a woman staying in an abusive relationship today! Today's Christian leaders need to understand the extra trap that Christian women are caught in, in addition to all the reasons given in part two. They should also realise their own limitations and not be afraid to encourage women to the use secular services and local programmes, and to advertise these.

Having said this, it is also important that leaders familiarise themselves with basic information as to the types of services that are available for all vulnerable people, so that they can pass them on to the relevant professional bodies, as well as giving support themselves.

I struggle with all advertising that promises we can end mass inhumanity to man in any context, and include domestic violence in this, but if the Church exposes it as unacceptable we can be the ones to start to make a difference both now and in the future. The Church needs to get to grips with the issues surrounding domestic violence – all of them, even the more unsavoury ones; they need to take it seriously. As well as this they need to look for telltale signs, investigate them with sensitivity, confront the offending partner (when it is safe to do so without putting the woman at risk), discipline the perpetrator, not as a punitive, but rather a corrective measure in order to express the Church's attitude to such behaviour. After all, the Church speaks out about practically everything else; and, if we were speaking about 'adultery' – does the Church consider this to be a 'private' matter?

I have been very open and honest throughout in both positive and negative experiences in finding myself as a Christian in this situation. I have to say that many non-Christian friends were initially very impressed at my church's loving reaction, but later felt let down with me, particularly when my support network fell away for a time. But we are all human, we all make mistakes; I have given, in my distress, mixed messages so that some of their actions were actually, they thought, in accordance with my wishes. It was a new pastoral experience to them, if not a totally new problem, and they have slowly grown and moved along the path with me. People have admitted in retrospect that mistakes have been made and that things will be different for women of the future. Whilst it has caused me extra suffering at times to have been almost a 'guinea pig', it makes my story and my suffering worthwhile because we have all learned and grown together and my church is moving towards that visible goal of being a safe haven for women who've been abused, and if I have inadvertently helped that process then I hope I have changed the future for some women, and for the church's outlook in general. It is hard to say that anything makes my recent sufferings 'worth it', but I am confident that there will be a time when I can look back and be thankful that I have played a part in a small, but potentially life-saving ministry. We should not be tempted to over criticise the Church; no one in my situation, perpetrator aside, has ever claimed to have 'got it right'- we know we have all been on a steep learning curve together.

And what has got me through this has been my faith first, my family, my church, my friends, and even specialists and counselling services very much second, because it is only in Christ alone that I can come to terms with what has happened and grow back into me, and move on through those years that have been missed out through violence. I lived for years in the most demeaning situation, have tolerated insults, and abuse, not realising I was undermining my own self-respect. Respect cannot exist in an atmosphere of abuse. The more you allow yourself to be insulted, the more you increase your own sense of hurt and humiliation. A violent home is a fearful home and I often feel that memories can never go completely away because they form you and mould you into the person you become. As a Christian I want God to have more control in my life than Rob, than my thoughts and self-hatred and the person Rob portrayed me as being. I know I can win the race with God - and that although the past will always form part of my life, I will let God be in control of those memories - they will not control me. That is healing. That is when I can really say the words of the song, and mean it: "For as He stands in victory, sin's curse has lost its grip on me … no power of hell, no scheme of man, can ever pluck me from His hands, till He returns or calls me home, here in the power of Christ, I live."

My great thank goes to the Baptist Union of Great Britain, along with the Worldwide Council of Churches who are doing some fantastic work in raising awareness of domestic violence amongst church leaders, and have allowed me to reproduce some of their material here.

The Baptist Union of Great Britain is committed to learning what it means to follow Jesus in a violent world. In partnership with others, they want to help break the silence surrounding domestic violence, and it is with this charter in mind I want to look at this issue further.

The following is from 'It Doesn't Happen Here', pack of the Baptist Union of Great Britain.

Following Jesus in a Violent World

Domestic violence: a charter for churches

Violence against women in all its forms is unacceptable in the church and in society. The Baptist Union Council:

1. Resolves to work towards making all our churches safe places where women who have experienced abuse can find sanctuary and informed help.
2. Commends the guidelines 'It Doesn't Happen Here' for use in churches in membership of the Baptist Union of Great Britain.
3. Urges every local congregation to break the silence over domestic violence.

CHARTER

This Church:

1. Accepts that domestic violence occurs in church families as well as in wider society, and is unacceptable in all its

forms.

2. Undertakes to listen, support and care for those affected by domestic violence.
3. Will keep up to date with the support agencies locally available, and will publicise them. We will also learn from them and work with them inappropriate ways.
4. Will play its part in teaching that domestic violence is a sin, requiring repentance, before reconciliation with God and the victim can occur.
5. Will live a new model of what it means to be human, male and female, both made in God's image. We will teach and preach this, thereby challenging society and affirming that God is a God of love, justice, mercy and forgiveness.
6. Will seek to appoint someone to encourage the use of good practice guidelines, and to keep the Church informed about the implementation, review and development of this charter.

This charter for churches was written initially by the Women's Group of the Gloucestershire churches together, and shared as a statement for local churches to use.

> *"The church must accept that domestic violence is a crime. It refers to a pattern of violent and controlling behaviour by one adult in an intimate relationship with another. It may include repeated physical abuse, or take the form of sexual or psychological threats or abuse and control. Verbal abuse, even alone, can be very powerful. The most harmful abuse is carried out by men against female partners, but can also occur by women against men, and in same-sex relationships. It is rarely a one-off event, and is more common than most people realise.*
>
> *Women who have been abused, whether physically, or sexually, emotionally or mentally, do not ask for help easily. There are still so many myths around, perpetuated often unwittingly by attitudes in society towards women,*

that make it incredibly difficult to ask for help. It may be difficult for someone of either sex who has been abused to be able to acknowledge that it is not their own fault, that it is not something they have done that causes the violence to happen. And so the violence becomes hidden, the victim becomes in some ways invisible, and often to be invisible each occasion when we failed to listen to words barely spoken, or just hinted at, or each time we unwittingly turned away, we add another layer to those already making the victim invisible. Unless we are acutely aware, we shan't ask the right questions, or create the right atmosphere in which it is possible to speak or ask.

The first steps are always to ensure safe boundaries, to ensure someone of confidentiality, to believe what is being said and to give priority to their safety.

It may be that someone is only able to break the silence much later, and now needs to work through how to pick up the pieces, to be free to get on with the rest of their life. The role of the church then is to continue the journey alongside the individual, respecting their decisions, and supporting them in their life choices.

Good practice guidelines

An advocate is someone who speaks for those who cannot easily express their views and feelings, and may not be taken into account in the ordinary business of church life. We may be familiar with appointing a children's advocate in the local church, in conjunction with the 'safe to grow' guidelines. The impetus for promotion of an advocate for those damaged by domestic abuse comes from the issues raised by the 'decade to overcome violence', accompanied by an increasing awareness in government and society that domestic violence is a serious crime.

Ideally, an advocate will:

- *Become a voice for victims and survivors, in considering how the church functions as an inclusive community and provides pastoral care.*

- *Act as a contact person for concerns regarding domestic violence, and maintain links with the community services.*
- *Support and monitor implementation and use of guidelines concerning domestic violence.*

First steps for the local church

- *Form a group (e.g. two or three women plus one man) to help the church to address domestic violence issues.*
- *Display posters and leaflets which offer information about help which is available for women.*
- *Place domestic violence hotline cards in pews or other suitable locations. Remember it is important for people to be able to access material discreetly, without embarrassment.*
- *Encourage those who lead worship to speak out against domestic violence in their teaching, preaching and prayers.*
- *Offer a marriage preparation and ongoing sessions for couples which addresses the themes of equality, conflict, violence and control.*
- *Designate a special day each year when the church will focus on developing awareness about domestic violence issues.*
- *Ensure that children and young people's programmes contain regular opportunities to look at anger management and violence in ways appropriate to their age and stage of development.*
- *Give financial support to the local domestic violence agency or refuge.*
- *Pay for the church leaders to attend training sessions on the pastoral care of those who have experienced domestic violence.*

Do's and don'ts in dealing with domestic violence

- *DO ensure her immediate safety. She will not be able to talk or think clearly if she is afraid.*
- *DO believe her. She is far more likely to minimise the problem than to dramatise it.*

- *DO recognise her need for positive response and support, even if there is nothing practical that you can do immediately.*
- *DO be sensitive to and discuss her fears about approaching the police. She may never have done so, or she may have done so many times and is hesitant to do so yet again.*
- *DO reinforce that we all expect to live free from violence. No one should have to live with violence in their own home. Violence is not an appropriate way to communicate within a relationship.*
- *DO make sure she knows how to contact the police and reach the local refuge where she can talk to workers even if she decides not to move in.*
- *DO reassure her that the violence her partner commits is his responsibility, and he should not blame her for his actions. He is the only one who has control over his behaviour.*
- *DO remember that if she is from an ethnic minority group, her problems could be compounded by racist reactions, language and cultural barriers, or fragile immigration status.*
- *DO always check that it will be safe to contact her at home should it become necessary. Do respect her wishes if she does not want you to make any contact. Her partner is unlikely to know that she has been to see you about the violence, and it is even less likely to take kindly to it. Confidentiality is crucial.*
- *DO find out what she wants to do and see if you can help achieve it. Consult with specialist agencies for individuals and see what they can offer. Inaccurate advice can increase her danger.*
- *DO recognise that it can take a victim years to leave a violent relationship.*
- *DO encourage her to be angry as this can be a useful catalyst that can mobilise her into taking action. Allow her to get in touch with her anger and let her know that her feelings are justified, and that expressing them is okay.*

What not to do

- *DON'T ask her what she did to provoke the violence. If you do, you are implicitly condoning his actions.*
- *DON'T suggest that she should try again. She has probably been doing that for a long time now. Once violence has become part of the relationship it will not go away. There is a lot of evidence to show that violent incidents increase in severity and become more frequent over time.*
- *DON'T suggest any combined interview. She may feel too threatened to speak freely in the presence of her assailant, and responsibility for the violence can become lost in justifications etc. If she does speak out, the repercussions afterwards may be serious.*
- *DON'T expect her to make a binding decision in a hurry. Many women say that they wish to stay with their partner, and that they only want the violence to stop. This decision-making process can be assisted by your patient and long term support and encouragement. It may take years for a woman to make a final decision to leave.*
- *DON'T make decisions for her. It is up to her to decide if she wants to leave the man or give it another try. By all means discuss her options, but leave her to decide what fits best her situation.*
- *DON'T pass on information about her new home to anyone, without her specific permission.*
- *DON'T ignore your intuition!*

To choose to beat their partners, people must believe that one person is entitled to control and the other is required to obey. They must believe that a 'moral 'person may legitimately use violence against other members of the family.

Key points to remember in meeting with a victim:

- *Believe her.*
- *Take her story seriously.*
- *Tell her it was not her fault.*
- *Acknowledge her courage in telling you.*
- *Be aware that she or her children may be in danger.*
- *Remember any choices or decisions are hers.*
- *Stay alongside her.*
- *Keep calm.*
- *Accept your own limitations.*
- *Give her time and space.*
- *Assure her of confidentiality.*
- *Pray with her only if she asks or freely agrees."*

Victims of domestic violence do not nag, demand or neglect. They are far too frightened. In fact, they do everything in their way to pacify their partners in order to avoid another unprovoked assault. I have to say that I never remember an assault that was preceded by a real argument. And, even if a man were to be provoked, then violence is never an appropriate way of dealing with it. Responsibility for the violence rests entirely with the perpetrator.

"What can my local church do to raise awareness of domestic violence?

For many people in the church domestic violence is a taboo subject which 'we don't like to talk about'. But it is as likely that many in the church will know victims of violence will be victims or abusers themselves. It is important that the subject is on the church agenda.

As church members:

- *Encourage your worship leaders and ministers regularly to pray and preach about it as being unacceptable.*

- *Recognise that this may raise issues for those who hear – ensure that there is someone who will listen.*
- *Find out what helping agencies exist in the local community; publish their details on notice boards and in the church magazine.*
- *Invite speakers to church groups, including youth groups.*
- *Ensure pre-marriage counselling deals with the issues of conflict, control and the possibility of violence.*
- *Challenge inappropriate behaviour by church members.*
- *Respect people's wishes during greetings, sharing the peace etc.*

If you are a minister or church leader:

- *Do all you can to make church a safe environment.*
- *Encourage inclusive language.*
- *Avoid approaches to worship and church business which close down the possibilities for someone to speak of their experience of abuse."*

What about domestic violence in a Christian marriage?

In the Bible, domestic violence is only referred to explicitly on one occasion. Even way back in Old Testament times wives were recognised as worthwhile people, whose husbands were not allowed to injure, kill or sell them, as they were allowed to do with slaves. Whilst they were subject to their husbands, even back then their husbands did not own them, something that has implications for us today, many, many thousands of years on. Men who abuse women today are implying that they are possessions that they can treat as they please. Even in an Old Testament context it was unthinkable for a wife to be the object of violence. It was simply not part of ancient biblical thinking or culture. While she could be unfairly disposed of as a wife if she was slandered against, her husband was punished severely (Deuteronomy 22:13-19 Holy Bible).

The sixth Commandment says: "You shall not murder." (Exodus 20:13). These Commandments operate on the basis of the 'worst-case scenario', i.e. the greatest sin is forbidden and it therefore follows that lesser but related sins are forbidden too. God places a very high value on people's physical wellbeing, recognising that violence is an evil crime that screams for God's vengeance.

Relationships cannot survive without respect, and when the abuse is ongoing respect is lost. It is absolutely unbiblical for any marriage to be violent and just as unbiblical for a woman to stay in a home where violence is present. You have a Christian obligation to seek protection for yourself. Also in the Old Testament the husband was reduced to poverty and forced to work for her for the rest of his life. God places a high value on womanhood and on peace and harmony in a home. God does not just care about physical violence but also about verbal abuse, slander and insults, along with unpredictable and uncaring behaviour.

People often mention the first part of Malachi 2:16, which states God saying that He "hates divorce", but often failed to include the second part of the verse which says that He hates this as much as He hates violence. Violence breaks the marriage covenant, denounces the vows 'to have and to hold ... till death parts us', and means that a normal marriage cannot exist as it has become a mockery - with no basis for the marriage left. As a Christian woman you still have no right to remain in such a demeaning marriage. It is important to pray and to keep the family together, but God's law 'you shall not commit murder' must come first. Domestic violence breaks this rule, along with self-image, self-respect, emotional wellbeing and the right to grow up in safety and peace being murdered as well.

God neither condones violence nor expects women to endure it. The whole root of domestic violence is that abusers are not living to the principles laid out in the Bible, which promote equal, non-violent relationships, although there is, of course, always the message of hope for abusers.

We are made in God's image, and domestic violence makes a mockery of this, and women must be aware that they are not the first to break the marriage vows. The very first time a man abuses a woman, the marriage vows are broken, whether the abuse is emotional, physical, sexual or psychological. In a Christian marriage, particularly, there is a covenant, whereby the husband loves his wife as Christ loves the Church. This verse can be easily misinterpreted today by people who do not understand, making it sound as though it is leading to inequality - in fact the opposite is true; Jesus loves us in an all embracing, totally self-sacrificial way, which leads in human relationships to total interdependence, which should then be reflected by husband and wife.

***So what makes a Christian woman stay in a Christian relationship*?**

Apart from all the other things mentioned in other chapters, Christian women have other difficulties to face. Some other things that come to my mind as an abused woman are listed below.

- Will people in the church believe me?
- What about my husband's role in the church?
- How will mutual friends cope?
- Will the church be supportive of me?
- What will happen if my husband wants to worship at the same church?
- Will I still have a social life, seeing as much of it exists around church people?
- Because in retrospect, I now realise I was being abused before we were married, should I stay in the marriage almost as a punishment for my foolishness?
- Should I stay to keep order, to provide a role model of

spiritual maturity to a much younger Christian?

- Jesus suffered for me, therefore should I stay and suffer in order to share in his sufferings?
- Should I stay as some sort of spiritual sacrifice?
- Should I stay because I have promised to be here "for better or for worse" and "till death us do part"?
- Should I try harder, because as a Christian I am always wanting to become more like Jesus, and if I was more like Jesus maybe this wouldn't be happening to me? (Don't know why I ever thought this; Jesus was perfect and look what happened to him!!)
- Does it look unforgiving if I leave?
- Is it a bad witness to others?

I could go on, the list is endless! It has taken me a long time to realise that suffering denies me full life. Jesus wants me to live positively, not suffering or being abused. Suffering for someone else must also be an act of free choice, and I did not choose to suffer.

> *"Where it is inflicted on an unwilling victim, then as with Jesus's own suffering, we cry 'this is unjust'. Jesus did not seek suffering; he rebelled against it even on its threshold. Losing your life in order to save it (Luke 9:24) expresses the paradox at the heart of our faith, but it should not be taken out of the context of the whole of Jesus's life. It should never be used as a justification of violence of abuse against women, and women should be encouraged to read the scriptures in a way that affirms their identity and their gifting." (Praying Our Goodbyes)*

Women need to be helped to reposition God as loving creator, in His being as Trinity femaleness is fully integrated. It may sometimes be helpful for women see God as mother. To delight in the female in God is another way women can be helped to treasure themselves as made in God's image.

As Christians we are taught to forgive, and the church is

a place of forgiveness. I spoke with a magistrate who knew I was a Christian shortly after getting my injunction against Robert. She said to me, 'Watch the church, Vicky, it can be dangerous place for you, what with forgiveness and all that.' Of course forgiveness lies at the heart of the Gospel, and if it were not for forgiveness there would be no hope for any of us.

However, forgiveness often isn't, or can't be, offered until justice has been done. In the Bible it is always justice that comes first. I can honestly say that in order to stay sane I forgave Rob every evening before I went to bed. In some ways my healing process has been slowed by the fact that I find it still now extremely difficult to be angry with Rob, and much easier to be angry with those who are less deserving, for example, those at church, and in particular, myself. My anger has been and still remains mostly self-directed and it's possibly what has caused the most damage.

One of the most hurtful things has been when I asked to join a home group where small groups gather together for prayer, Bible study and fun, and I was pleased to see a new group just down the road from me, with all new people, therefore no reminders of Rob, something that has made going to church extremely difficult, and the opportunity to give and make new friends. I was told in no uncertain terms (admitted by the young leader) that there were already enough people with 'baggage' and that I should find somewhere else to go. Of course there are many loving and extremely welcoming and great groups out there, but I have to travel and I have a disability as well. But after I requested this I got a DVD sent to me about forgiveness and revenge. Although a very small minority, there are still those whose pride will not allow them to access the information offered on domestic violence and who seek to speak in riddles and judge rather than take me to one side to see how I am doing. They claim to know how I am and yet an unexplained move (which to this day I don't understand and for which I have never yet received either an apology or explanation) could potentially have led me to take my own life. People are mysterious beings, and yet most of us are gregarious by nature. The following are extremely important points to remember when dealing with anyone who has been through such trauma and has such complex needs which must be taken seriously. Sensitivity must lie at the heart of all our dealings with the abused, no matter how repetitive or 'stuck' the difficulties seem to have become. Remember the part rejection has already played and the healing power of acceptance.

The low self-esteem which abuse of any sort engenders is so demoralising. The journey to wholeness is a long one, and has so many ups and downs, both for the survivor, and for those who accompany her on the journey. During this time, as you know, any woman is especially vulnerable, and things which appear to be disregard or injustice quite unintentionally will so easily make her fall back into the emotions of low esteem caused by the abuse.

We must always be careful about asking people who have been abused to forgive, without knowing how they are going on the journey, while at the same time recognising that forgiveness does bring healing.

It should be emphasised that forgiveness is not an event but another journey. So often with an expectation of someone else forgiving, people can add to our sense of burden of sin and failure if we have not reached that stage on the journey, especially so when it is us who have faced the abuse and not those trying to help us.

Anyone trying to help must firstly speak regularly to the woman in order to gauge what kind of emotional and physical state she is in, and indeed to even fully know the background of what has and is actually happening to her at that moment.

Forgiveness and anger are not incompatible emotions, and forgiveness and justice are certainly not incongruous, as we learn from the Lord Himself.

Several people from my church have spontaneously said

that if I love Rob then I should have taken action before, and numerous Christian police officers have been quite cross when I have asked for advice, wondering why on earth a professing Christian should get away with violence in marriage twice.

I was hesitant to share details with the church initially, partly through not wanting to betray Rob, and partly because I saw how much it had hurt and damaged my friends, but eventually I decided it was necessary for the main group of leaders to know, not just for me, but so that other women didn't have to necessarily go through all the explanations for themselves. I finally explained that what I was struggling with at that point was reliving death threats numerous times a day, seeing Rob everywhere - a smell, a sight, a memory, a sound will bring back that thought of having been kicked on the floor with pint glasses smashed over your head, but not being able to see because spasms have forced your neck back into an 'easy to strangle' position and your eyes clamped shut, and the phone being moved to prevent you calling 999. I explained that these flashbacks had got to the point where I have passed out and gone into shock so I can't drive anywhere, or go to work.

Many women, especially as most of us have been called 'mad' or 'crazy', are particularly sensitive when we realise that we have changed, albeit temporarily, and are acting in ways that may seem irritable, disrespectful or obsessive.

And, thinking further about forgiveness - imagine, if you can, being held as a hostage - maybe handcuffed, tied up, weapons lying all around. Do you actually think the terror would allow any feelings of resentment or unforgiveness? And once you had escaped, just think seriously; would these still be emotions high on the agenda - no, in fact when I was rescued, the whole irony is that I felt guilty that I had survived, because that meant people knowing - and I felt I was betraying Rob. Of course this is not betraying - I know from my minister's words that Rob was one hundred per cent responsible for every ounce of his behaviour and for breaking our vows, but it doesn't feel like that. In fact, although I have had many sessions with outreach services, and some with a post-traumatic stress psychologist and counsellors, I still continue to have feelings of guilt and shame. I am starting to feel slightly angry at times, but I cannot allow myself to be angry at Rob – it just turns inwards and I feel this is the one of the reasons for my depression.

I have said to the church that I don't want to 'air my dirty laundry' in public, and maybe even these details given were too explicit for some (although only a very sketchy outline of what I have been through), but asked for them to be aware that in our church there will be at least ten other women statistically who are facing abuse to some degree behind closed doors. Remember they may well already have that deep forgiveness that others may know nothing about because they've never had anything so serious to forgive. Prayerful discernment and relevant factual information is crucial in handling all these situations.

Sometimes I have felt that if I was more like Jesus then maybe in response to all injustices, whether intended or not, I should be silent as "a sheep before its shearers" – but I have also been reminded of how He overturned the money tables and shouted in righteous indignation. For those times when I have been misunderstood, I can only say with great humility: 'Father forgive, because they don't know what they're doing.'

My church has yielded to me some extraordinarily loving people, but these are the people who have always known me or have made the trouble to get alongside me in my hour of need.

It is vital to find people who will draw alongside women with compassion and true insight rather than sending, as happened to me just the once, riddles from a distance that left me guessing, which neither helped my psychiatric injuries or edified me spiritually.

I am praying that what I have been through is for a reason that will one day be revealed, maybe initially it is to help guide churches and their leadership to be informed, prayerful and discerning on an issue that does exist within its membership, and needs addressing with acute sensitivity.

Justice has been on my mind a lot recently. I want Rob to face the sort of justice that is restorative in order so that he can live a fulfilled life, and in order for him not to reoffend, which, all the time he remains in denial, I am absolutely certain that he will. The police have recently confirmed that the even the 'smaller' incidents which have become part of normal life, are actually GBH. When they told me, I laughed – I seriously thought they were joking. It frightens me how used you can get to being treated in a certain way. Once I knew that Rob's actions towards me were so serious, I backtracked with the police for several months. It wasn't until I got my Bible out (my legalistic personality means that, until I lost my support network, I read it every day of my life, even though on occasions it doesn't go in) after about six weeks, and it opened on the page that said, "Have nothing to do with the fruitless deeds of darkness, but rather, expose them," (Holy Bible Ephesians 5 v II) that I knew that God's will sometimes involves us leaving or even leading our abuser into the hands of justice. But that is a whole new story ...

I have learnt quite a few things about forgiveness recently and one is that forgiveness is not being walked over, it is not carrying on being a victim of an abusive behaviour. Being willing to forgive does not mean tolerating dysfunctional behaviour or passively accepting disloyalty from trusted friends or abuse from family members or malpractice from professional workers. I can forgive my husband who abused me but I do not have to stick around to put up with more of the same. I can forgive professional workers whose thoughtlessness or naivety caused me pain, but I don't have to put up with all the injustice arising from it if there is something that I can do about it. Basically what I think I am trying to say is that forgiveness is not the same as allowing people to be irresponsible for their own actions.

When I took out the injunction, I really thought that Rob would immediately call out to God, break down in tears and see the error of his ways, and that then everything would be better and we would be the 'and we all lived happily ever after' story that I introduced in my foreword. But it was not be. All indications are that he has just gone further and further into self-denial. I have to stop myself thinking that this is my fault, that I have failed him yet again.

What about anger?

After seventeen months I am just beginning to be able to explore my own anger at all that has happened to me, which is a very positive stage after years of feeling that I mustn't get angry; something which we so often learn from our childhood up, and I hope I will be able to use this creatively rather than negatively, turning it inwards as I so often have done and still have a tendency to do. I have really struggled with anger. Next to self-esteem it's been the most difficult thing. I think, having dealt with this topic a great deal recently, that the two are linked. They are linked because if I am angry at Rob I have to then deal with it, and put it away from my thoughts - lock it up in the box of thoughts I'm not allowed to unlock. For some people, doing this would leave them some happy memories of good times shared together that were not abusive. But for me there would be nothing left. If I am angry with Rob, and deal with this, and lock those thoughts away, then he will be gone, out of my life - forever. Much as I loved him, still do, there simply are so few times to remember that he may as well have never come into my life. And I'm not ready for that - yet.

It is actually good and healthy to show anger - God promotes anger if it's justified - it's how you act it out that matters. When I think of anger, I can only think of violence. It was helpful to be asked about my parents and how they reacted when they were angry with me as a child - they must have been angry with me – I know they were, frequently – I've checked! But I find it difficult to remember the loving anger that meant they expressed it calmly, gently, in words. It helped me when I was told by a keyworker that it made her angry when I use derogatory words about myself. I still can't quite grasp how someone can be angry without me noticing or flinching or feeling frightened, but they can – it's an indignation about something that is inappropriate.

It's okay to shout and scream or even to smash a harmless object when you feel angry about abuse. It took me months before I could see the point in getting angry in a constructive way rather than in a way that caused me either physical or emotional pain so that I could actually feel the anger. I had to feel it, rather than just experience it. That's destructive anger – like Rob's actually – but it's a stage of post-traumatic stress that is not unusual. I have been frightened of being angry, frightened that I'll be out of control or consumed by it if I really start to feel it. I also know that if I sit on it, it will fester inside and turn into bitterness or resentment and change me. Whilst I was still with Rob I had daily panic attacks. I realise now that was internalised rage – that was because I wasn't allowed to express it. Now I can – and I can't! It is important to remember that any repressed anger makes illness worse.

The Bible says anger is okay. It's what it can lead to that may be wrong. It is right to be angry about unfairness and wrongs. The question is 'How can I express anger rightly without hurting anyone?' Often, when you acknowledge a feeling it loses some of its power. It is frightening to feel anger if you haven't felt it much before. Often, if injustices are put right then the cause of the anger disappears, and this can be another reason for cooperating with legal bodies to ensure that justice is done.

But can God change abusers?

God is the God of miracles, and therefore He can do

anything. However, especially once it has been pointed out to him, the man must want to change his abusive ways. It has been a hard lesson for me to learn, as I thought that today I would be sitting here with the man I love suddenly fulfilling everything I needed in him as a husband. I don't know whether you call this naivety or hope – it's not really worth bothering about anymore. I do know that whatever happens Rob and I will never be together again, although I still don't know how I will physically sign our divorce papers. But I can hope and pray that he seeks help and that he finds wholeness and healing, and a special role to fulfil in both his secular and spiritual life.

Having spoken to both secular and Christian counsellors, they all say the same thing – that men do not change. From a Christian perspective, God can heal. However, we are still physical beings and in our weaker moments we all resort to our greatest weakness, and in the case of an abuser, this is violence; so I have learned one very sad thing – that I will never be safe with Rob.

Whilst Christians may feel reconciliation should always be a goal, in cases of domestic violence it is always better to save a life than save a marriage.

Until the imbalance of power and control is challenged and worked through professionally, the perpetrator will continue his abusive behaviour. The Christian perpetrator who claims that a lack of self-control is causing his behaviour needs to consider just how much of his life has really been surrendered to God, as one of the fruits of the spirit is 'self control'.

Christian men who have been violent often feel remorseful. But it is the job of Christian leaders to look for true signs and fruit of repentance and be aware that deception and 'false fronts' are all part of the cycle of power and control. It is important to remember that his outward public appearance doesn't necessarily mean that he has changed. Church workers need to exercise great wisdom and discernment when dealing with perpetrators; in most cases only time (and usually a very long time) will demonstrate that an abuser has turned away from his violent behaviour.

As a Christian I do believe that God can change dramatically and quickly because I've seen it in other situations. However, men must always be encouraged to turn to experienced agencies who are involved in working with perpetrators and one sign of true repentance is that they will be willing to do this. The Church has the potential to shape people for life, to influence values and attitudes of individuals. The Church's message and example should be Christ-centred, where men are encouraged to live the Biblical message of 'maleness'. I remember being very moved by a sermon I heard in church whilst I was still with Rob – where gentleness was described as 'power under control'.

Never forget that each person is accountable for the choices they make and the actions they take. Perpetrators aren't to blame for the social forces that portray 'maleness' as the very opposite to the Bible, but they are to blame for their individual actions. Before God, the perpetrator's argument or excuse that society or background are to blame for his abuse will not stand, and without repentance he will be condemned for his behaviour in abusing his partner.

Christian leaders should communicate God's hatred and condemnation of violence, demonstrated by society, and communicate the value God places on both women and men.

The Church must also recognise that wittingly or unwittingly they (but not the Bible) have perpetuated the myth of male supremacy over the years, and need to repent of this, asking forgiveness for generations of men who have oppressed and dominated women over the years. I hold strongly to the Biblical principle of different gender roles in the church, but recognise that in the past centuries some teaching has been unhelpful by inadvertently promoting inequality.

The Church needs to return to God's intended equality for men and women. When Jesus was on earth, he challenged the stereotypical culture of his time by stressing monogamy, he rebuked women for their social conformity, he included women in his entourage, and, in a society that barely recognised women, Jesus broke the mould by appearing to women after his resurrection. The apostle Paul says that we are all "one in Christ." Galatians 3 v 28.

Reconciliation and Restoration

Restoration, when it does happen, is a slow and arduous process. Whilst it is always a goal for a Christian, it does not, under any circumstance, mean encouraging a woman to either stay or return to an abusive cycle where the man has not recognised his faults and turned away from his old lifestyle. Reconciliation means that the perpetrator must do everything required to ensure that there is never a return to the former destructive and abusive lifestyle of the past.

Reconciliation means recognising and repenting of the sins against the victim(s) and against God. It means a strong resolve, even under pressure, to remain self-controlled and also the relearning of behaviour that excludes violent and abusive reactions and the need to exert control over others.

The Church needs to be aware of this process and not be naive in thinking everything will be okay after a prayer!

Reconciliation is a two-way process, however. A woman should take action against their abuser which may require telling someone official and/or leaving the perpetrator. Those women brave enough to take action are statistically, long term, less likely to be abused again (although the most dangerous time for a woman is immediately after taking action). Fear should no longer be in control with women being encouraged to take control of their own lives. The pattern of forgiveness isn't letting the perpetrator off the hook. Luke 17 v 3,4 makes it clear that it is biblical to hold the abuser to account for his behaviour, therefore reminding him of the path he has chosen to walk away from.

It should also be noted that there is a difference between

repentance, i.e. a complete acknowledgement and turning around, and regret, i.e. wishing you hadn't behaved in a certain way because of the trouble it got you into. For example, 2 Cor 7 v 9–11 says: "For you became sorrowful as God intended and so were not harmed in any way by us. Godly sorrow brings repentance that leads to salvation. See what this Godly sorrow has produced in you - what earnestness, what eagerness to clear yourselves, what indignation, what alarm, what longing, what concern, what readiness to see justice done."

Remember that perpetrators often try to win back their victims by showing tenderness or showering her with gifts. Remember the trap that victims are in because they so want to believe their abuser has changed. A perpetrator may become very responsive to their victim's needs and often trap them all over again. Romans 6 v 18: "For such people are not serving the Lord, but their own appetites. By smooth talk and flattery they deceive the minds of naive people."

Church leaders must constantly be looking for the signs of real and ongoing change in a person. Seek to establish a relationship of strict accountability, where a designated person can ask him regularly how he is coping and establish a trusting relationship so that he can confide if he feels that he may abuse again.

The Church and both parties

The traditional teaching of the church remains true: that marriage is sacred, and divorce, on the whole, an unacceptable option. However, pastoral responsibility always lies with the one who has come to you for help: in the majority of cases, the abused women.

> *"Women are often reluctant to turn to the Church for advice because they are afraid that they will be taught to pray harder to make the marriage work, or to avoid aggravating her partner.*

She is also likely to have struggled with her spiritual understanding of what is happening to her: for example, God is testing her but will never let her bear more than she can handle.
Or, God is calling her to save her husband.

As abused women we may be questioning faith in a God who seems to condone the situation. We may begin to think that God sees us and criticises us in the same way as our husbands. We may be full of guilt and self-loathing. We have become someone unworthy of life and approval, however hard we try to earn both. God and our husbands are on the same side, and we are left out and alone.

Of course this is not true but this is so deep and complex that simply to tell her that God loves her is not enough. To tell her that the church loves her and is praying for her is also not enough. I know. I've been there. (Even now I feel guilty and ungrateful in writing this, but this is not a criticism, it is an attempt to educate.) *A woman may now mistrust and reject the Bible, and the God she has worshipped for years. Her greatest immediate need will be for friends to accept and care for her, offering a different image of God's opinion of her. It may be a slow process, as trust is built up. You can help open up opportunities for her to develop friendships, so that this might involve such highly spiritual activities as visits to the hairdresser and shopping for new clothes! If you are a man, she has come to you for help, and so you will be part of the new image she is building up, but you will also need to find support for her in a trusted woman friend, or elder/deacon.*

Do not automatically expect her to come to church as this may be impossible for her.

At one level, when her husband is not a Christian you may feel this simplifies the situation. You may know him, and may well have been praying for him. Continue to do so, but never see that becoming a Christian will solve problems in the marriage. At this point in their relationship, discussion of marriage to a non-

Christian, or to one who has left the church, detracts from the real issue – that of abuse. Never forget who is the victim and who is the abuser. He cannot be excused or his behaviour condoned in any way just because he is not a Christian. In practical terms, pastoral guidelines still apply.

What about the Christian perpetrator?

One of the hardest situations pastorally is when both victim and perpetrator are known to you as members of the church fellowship. You may be shocked by what you have heard and find it hard to believe. You may also feel both anger and grief. When the victim has come to you, your pastoral responsibility is always to her.

You must not talk with a perpetrator about what you have heard in an attempt to bring about a reconciliation. Such a move, however well intentioned, is an act of betrayal of someone who has put a trust in you. To talk to her partner would be to place her at risk.

It is well known that perpetrators will minimise what has happened as a one-off occurrence, or as a gross exaggeration of a reasonable or normal disagreement, or as a hysterical invention of an emotionally disturbed individual. It would be so easy to think that this is the truth." **This is particularly so in the case of women who have recently escaped and are consequently suffering from the symptoms of post-traumatic stress disorder**. *"Perpetrators who are members of the church fellowship and even respected church workers are no different from others in this respect. It is also known that on average, women do not speak of abuse until up to thirty incidents have taken place, and that they are at the greatest risk when they first summon up the courage to speak to someone, or make an attempt to leave. It is also easy to say that this is something they must talk through and sort out between themselves. But by the time someone has talked to you, this is dangerous advice.*

Only when you know that she is safe, and that further action is possible, and you have her permission to speak, can you act. Once other agencies become involved, some action may be essential. The perpetrator may need an advocate but that must not be you. You have to find someone else who can take on this role. It may be necessary to suspend him away from office or area of responsibility he holds in the church and to stay away from the church fellowship. The victim should not feel that she is the one who has to leave the church.

There are organisations to help perpetrators face up to, and acknowledge responsibility for, their actions and work for change. Change is not easy: responsibility is often denied and change resisted. Agreement to work for change may only come as a part of a court ruling or condition of probation. True repentance will recognise the need for change, the need to place their partner's wellbeing before their own, and to be prepared to accept that this may bring about life changes that are not what the perpetrator may have wished. This may include moving from the family home, seeing the children in supervised access, giving up church responsibilities, worshipping in a different fellowship. It should be noted that it is impossible to support both victim and perpetrator within the same fellowship." ('It Doesn't Happen Here')

And finally ...

If an abusive husband is not prepared to take responsibility for his actions and go through perpetrator programmes and reconciliation, then a wife should take legal action.

Old Testament divorce laws were a merciful provision and even though God hates divorce He indicates in Malachi 2v 16 that He would rather have this than He would have a woman abused. So, no woman married to a perpetrator is doing wrong if she seeks divorce.

Just as Jews understood the 'no work' laws could be set aside if an 'animal fell into a pit' so biblical exceptions should be made when people find themselves in danger. Jesus taught that sometimes the spirit of the law allows specific legal requirements to be overridden. (See 'It Doesn't Happen Here', Baptist Union Of Great Britain and Worldwide Council of Churches.)

Sometimes we need to break a relationship, to bid someone farewell. Pray for freedom. Pray for your abuser, your husband, partner, boyfriend.

> *"God of beginnings and end of endings, grant that I might have the strength to put an end to this matter which has weighed so heavily on my heart and my mind. Grant that I might bid farewell to this relationship which has brought me so much pain and grief. You know that this dying which is so evident in the process of termination will truly be a step into new life for me. I feel fragile and frail at this moment, even though I know it is the right direction and decision for me. Help me to close the door on this section of my journey, to walk into new rooms of life. I need to the experience a freshness and a vitality like a cool breeze of a spring morning coming through an open window. Be this vitality for me, God of compassion. Grant that I may turn my back and walk away from what has been. I pray that I may be healed of this hurt and I pray that any whom I have hurt through this experience may also be healed. Amen." (Praying Our Goodbyes)*

Prayer is an essential part of healing. God understands that for lengthy periods of time these prayers may simply be 'help'. God has sent me people from church who pray with me weekly, and I know many many more who pray for me every day. I can often feel when they're praying. Many people phoned me in the early days to tell me they were praying. One week, soon after the injunction, I received twenty calls from church (excluding my social group at the time) from people who said they were praying for me. Months later I know many of them still are. I often pray with tears not words, and I can thank my original keyworker for that, as once she taught me it was safe to cry (as my new one is teaching me that it's safe to be angry) I discovered, after a few 'practice runs', that tears are healing!

Jesus knew what it was to be perfectly loving yet totally

unwanted. Physically and emotionally he was made to feel shame on the cross. He understands shame. Yet he had nothing to be ashamed about as an innocent victim. His experiences were not comparable to anything any of us have suffered but he understands it so much more.

Sometimes it feels as though the joy of restoration is impossible and as if the process of healing will never end. But God's power to heal is infinite.

If I'm completely honest, just months ago it was impossible to believe that a restored life was possible. Now and again, and as I write this part I am only eight months on, it still is. However, with God all things are possible. As I wrote this last section my television was on in the background. I wasn't really even watching it - it was just company - and I was enjoying the control of having it on when I wanted and on what channel I wanted. Even the pleasure of not having to pluck up courage for two hours to ask if the volume could please be turned down was something I was revelling in. But just as I was 'enjoying' this, whilst simultaneously mourning my loss, these words suddenly caught my attention from the TV screen:

"O love, that will not let me go,
I rest my weary soul in You,
I give You back the life I owe,
that in Your ocean depths its flow
May richer, fuller be.

O joy that seekest me through pain,
I cannot close my heart to You;
I trace the rainbow through the rain,
and feel the promise is not vain
that morn shall tearless be.

O Cross that liftest up my head,
I dare not ask to fly from You;
I lay in dust life's glory dead,

And from the ground there blossoms red
Life that shall endless be."

(George Matheson 1842-1906)

"An Affirmation for women survivors

It happens everywhere
This is not God's will for you
it is not your fault
you are a valuable person who deserves a good life
you are not responsible for another person's violent or abusive behaviour
you do not have to tolerate, understand or accept it.
You deserve to find a safe person who will believe your story
you have the right to speak out about what has happened – when you choose to do so
you have the right to make choices and changes in your own life
there are others who have also suffered abuse in their lives, and yet have found a pathway to change
there are companions who are willing to share your struggle
together with others we can work to transform the relationships, attitudes and structures which are used to abuse and violate women."

by Lesley Orr. McDonald (Courtesy of BUGB)

And for all God's people everywhere – WE SAY 'YES'

To a world where all are valued for themselves
when no one is exploited or abused
where all can stand proud and strong
WE SAY 'YES'

To a church where healing and love embrace all
where there is acceptance of dissent and difference

where conformity gives way to the spirit of freedom
WE SAY 'YES'

To lives grounded in peace and justice
where struggle and self-acceptance walk in joy
where strength and tenderness join hands
WE SAY 'YES'

by Jan Berry (Courtesy of BUGB)

"For My grace is sufficient for you, for my power is made perfect through weakness ... for when I am weak, then I am strong." 2 Corinthians 12 v 9.

Epilogue – Today

A few months ago I sat with my sister's church in beautiful surroundings at their house party thinking about heaven. I was sitting next to my sister and her large bump who is thinking about entering the world as I write. On my lap, snuggled against me in my wheelchair (the one I need a little bit more than a few years ago, but was using for its comfort, and simply because I could without abuse), was my little niece, nearly three years old. I have, since that day back in 1999, found the song 'In Christ Alone' so intensely emotional that I have had to have 'toilet breaks' so that I can hear it from afar, as it's one of the many things that triggers the intrusive flashbacks of post-traumatic stress.

But something kept me there, that little person whose birth had coincided with my escape from denial.

I hoped she wouldn't look up at me, or feel the change in my breathing rate as the tears streamed down my face again as I held her tight and cast my mind back, knowing that "from life's first cry, to final breath, Jesus commands my destiny". It is no coincidence that, as I finish this part of my journey, her baby sister is, at this very moment of writing, at the very beginning of the journey from the womb to this earth. I knew back then that when I went home I wouldn't be facing the 'final breath' from the terror of domestic violence.

It's still only eighteen months since I got the injunction against Rob. But I don't know exactly how many months or days. I don't need to count anymore. I surprise myself when I think I haven't moved on and then go back and read my earlier writings.

Several people have commented on how, although I still suffer from the negatives, all the difficulties covered in this book, I am recently also talking about a future, and about choices. They are right – I hadn't noticed, the journey is so slow but so sure, it's sometimes tempting to remember only the negatives that are still happening, not the positives that are new. I can focus more often on the beginnings, not the ends, the "plans to prosper and not to harm ... plans for a hope and a future." (Jeremiah 11 v 29)

My body and my mind have finally given up running – just for now. I've been granted six months off work, to rest, to take proper care of myself, to make up for the fights of my now six and a half year journey. We had our fourth 'wedding anniversary' – in fact, Rob was arrested for ABH on that very day. As far as Rob is aware to date, the CPS have decided on 'no further action' because, although I had corroboration from Sharon and from all our local friends and family, because I didn't go to the doctors' with actual injuries until after the injunction it boiled down to my word against Rob's and I know I am not well enough to cope without special measures in court. These may still happen, since the CPS requested a forensic psychiatrist to assess me; she confirmed chronic post-traumatic stress, and that Rob was the definite cause of it. The case file is still showing as active. I do know, however, that should Rob lay a finger on another woman who is brave enough to go to the police it will show that there have been two women who have told their story before. I'm not changing my surname, although I'm not proud of it (at least it will die out with this generation!) – I'm more concerned for potential victims than I am for myself.

But I am learning not to worry about what's happening to him. I have tried and tried and tried to help him and it's all been rejected, but he may use it one day and I pray he will, but if not, what I am now fully convinced of is the fact that it's his choice, and his choice alone.

So, I can forget gradually about Rob, and think about

me. I have learned that even the best friends in the world sometimes need 'time out' and that this is not always wrong when they can come back to their original promises, although it may be hurtful at the time. I have always known I don't have 'fair weather' friends, and people's friendships will continue to help me in increasingly interdependent relationships. I have also learned that it's not wrong sometimes to sit and be given to – I have always been on the other side, and it's not wrong to take every now and again. I can remember a past where I have given and look to a future where I can give again.

I had a special 'unwedding' ceremony, just myself, my minister and his wife. I placed my rings on the table where I had stood and said my vows, the ones Rob broke, not me, as a symbol of giving back to God the pain, and the hopes of what could have been and now won't be – well, not with Rob anyway. It stopped the flashbacks in church immediately, although there are always other triggers to be worked through one by one. I belong to a new small church group, full of wonderful, caring people who have completely changed my life in the short time I have joined them. I have even hosted it and plan to take my turn in leading it. I have no problem in joining discussions and have to keep reminding the real me to be quiet every now and again!

I am fortunate in that I have fought for a specialist post-traumatic stress counsellor to help me for as long as necessary to work through similar things such as this.

Sometimes I think that I haven't got a clue as to what God would have me do with the rest of my life. I went to visit another local church last week – the first person I bumped into was a wonderful lady who used to go to my own church. The first thing she asked was, 'Is your husband with you?' I replied, 'No, he's not, as in, not at all.' God meant me to be there then. He meant me to be with someone who could understand and meet another supportive person, reminding me that His church, His people are everywhere and that His encouragements can be found all around, sometimes when we are least expecting them. And with this dear lady I pray that God will eventually take away all the memories that haunt me and are still so raw. But I also pray that through my life He will send women across my path and that, as a healed person, I will still be able to understand, to empathise, to look back at that scar which isn't going to bleed again however much it's picked, but will still be there to remind me of what's underneath, so that I can help others and then put the pain away, at the back of my memories where it belongs, and can work only for good and not bad.

I am still living in our house. It's all new and redecorated on a shoestring and looks just as good. I avoid 'our' bedroom, and I still need to get rid of that headboard with the heart in the middle. I firmly believe that I will be sharing it again one day and that my heart will be totally entwined with someone else's - but only God knows that, and it's not the right time for Him to reveal those plans yet. There are some parts of closure which I need to do myself. First I need to get rid of everything that is in my life now and start afresh. I want to move house (I won't move area on principle; that's just what Rob would expect me to do even though he is currently still a mile down the road, because all the time I'm in this house there can be no complete closure - Rob's handiwork is everywhere). I have heard he isn't buying down here in Devon though. But what's so great is, apart from any intervention of God's, I'll move *when I* want to, *where I* want to, *in my time*, not in Rob's.

I've been a respite carer for eleven years. I know that I still want to be a mother over everything else. I want to adopt if I don't marry again ...or maybe if I do.

I might downsize. Most people upgrade to have kids. But I want my children to have less money and more of me. I want them to have as much as they can, but material things are an optional extra. I want them to have me and my love. When I look at Rob and some materialistic friends he so loved to compete with, I feel actively proud of my desire to have a smaller property; it's one of the few things that's made me feel I actually have more than those friends. I don't need to do it – it's a choice. There's nothing emotionally I won't give my family, however it arrives with me!

And since I started this book I also have a church that is more understanding of the issues surrounding domestic violence. I am well aware that I am not the first, and sadly not the only or the last, but, I hope, the most annoying (!), the most persistent, the most pushy in informing them that we are not 'baggage'; we need ongoing help, support and understanding. I have always had the love and support, but education needs to be ongoing and at least it has started and is mentioned in church and in small groups. I am part of my church family, a body. I always was, but now I feel it again. There are a few who disapprove; I can count four that I know of, which isn't bad in a church of five hundred – and my minister, quite rightly, says I can choose to allow myself to be a victim of those people who just ignore me and don't matter, or I can get on with the other four hundred and ninety who love me! Bridges are constantly and consistently rebuilt, and I can let it be more 'their problem' and no longer mine.

The lady I met the other Sunday was talking to me about Ezekial 47, where God guides and protects – water is a great symbolism, especially for me, because it was used so often to abuse, but God uses it to show his protection and comfort; firstly when the waters are around our ankles, then our thighs, then our waists, then right up to our necks; but, like my physiotherapist in the water, even when my spasms are causing my body to thrash around, she will never let me go under. And I can never go completely under, not with God's arms holding me up and moving me gently along. "For underneath are the everlasting arms." (Deuteronomy 33 v 27)

Addresses and Helplines

Refuge
2–8 Maltravers Street, London, WC2R 3EE
Tel: 0207 395 7700
National 24-hour helpline run between Refuge and Women's Aid: 0808 2000247
E-mail: info@refuge.org.uk
Website: www.refuge.org.uk
Refuge also provides dedicated outreach services to support women with practical and emotional issues and to help work out safety plans.

Women's Aid
PO Box 391, Bristol, BS99 7WS
Tel: 0117 944 4411
E-mail: wafe@wafe.co.uk
Website: www.womensaid.org.uk
This is a particularly comprehensive website and my thanks goes to them for allowing me to use quotes.
www.domesticviolencedata.org

www.homeoffice.gov.uk/crime/domesticviolence/index.html

Domestic Violence Intervention Project (For perpetrators.)
PO Box 2838, London, W6 9ZE
Tel: 0208 748 6512

Shelterline (Helps with emergency housing and access to refuge services.)
Tel: 0808 800 444

Victim Support

Cranmer House, 39 Brixton Road, London 5W9 6DZ
Tel: 0845 3030900
Rights of Women
52-54 Featherstone Street, London, EC1Y 8RT
Tel: 0207 251 6575

The Samaritans
National Number: 08457 909090 (There are local branches too.)

NSPCC (For children.)
Tel: 0800 800 500 (This is free and is open 24 hours every day.)

Childline
Freepost 1111, London N1 OBR
Tel: 0800 1111

Baptist Union of Great Britain
Tel: 01235 517700 (Ministry section.)

Set Free (Christian)
PO Box 32, Kendal, Cumbria, LA9 4GF

Mind
Tel: 08457 660163

Careline
Tel: 0845 1228622 (Monday to Friday 10 a.m.-1 p.m., 7 p.m.-10 p.m.)

Crisis Service for Women
01179 251119 (Friday and Saturday 6-9 p.m., Sunday 9 p.m.-12.30 a.m.)

Rethink
Tel: 0845 4560455 (Mental health line.)

Saneline
Tel: 08457 678000

Supportline

Tel: 0208 5549004

Victim of Crime Trust
Tel: 08708 428467

Bibliography and Useful Reading

Joe and Liz Hayes, *Beaten, Battered, Bruised and Blessed* (Barrow-in-Furness: Self-Published, 1997).

Helen Conway, *Picking Up the Pieces: Coping with Domestic Violence* (Oxford: Lion Hudson PLC, 1997).

Meg Keenedy Dugan, *It's My Life Now* (USA: Mendocino College, 2002).

Joyce Rupp, *Praying Our Goodbyes* (Guildford: Eagle Press, 1988).

Pamela Reeve, *Faith Is* (USA: Multnomah Publishers, 1994)

Jill Brown, *What is This Place? – Bible Studies Exploring Issues Around Violence Against Women.*

Lundy Bancroft, *Why Does He Do That?* (USA: The Berkley Publishing Group, 2002).

'It Doesn't Happen Here' / *Breaking the Silence … On Violence Against Women* (Oxfordshire: Baptist Union of Great Britain / Churches Together in England / Worldwide Council of Churches, 2001)

Mary Marecek, *Breaking Free From Partner Abuse* (USA: Morning Glory Press, 1993).

David Kinchin, *Post Traumatic Stress Disorder – The Invisible Injury* (Oxfordshire: Success Unlimited, 2004).

Aruna Granadason, *The Church and Violence Against Women.*

Elaine Weiss, *Surviving Domestic Violence – Voices of Women Who Broke Free* (Agreka Books, 2001).

Ann Jones and Susan Schechter, *When Love Goes Wrong – What You Can Do When You Can't Do Anything Right* (USA: HarperPerennial, 1993).

Aphrodite Matsakis, *I Can't Get Over It – A Handbook for Survivors* (USA: New Harbinger Publications, 1996).